MW00416312

A NEW LOOK
AT THE
Old Testament

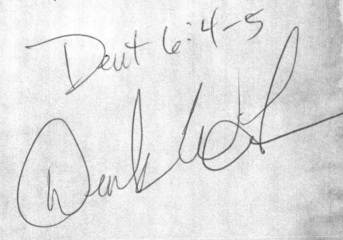

Deut 6:4-5

DEREK LEMAN

Mt. Olive
Press

A New Look at the Old Testament
by Derek Leman

Published by:
Mt. Olive Press
Post Office Box 659
Stone Mountain, GA 30086
mtolivepress.com

All rights reserved. No part of this book may be reproduced or transmitted in any form or by any means, electronic or mechanical, including photocopying, recording, or by any information storage and retrieval system, without written permission from the author, except for the inclusion of brief quotations in a review or as quotations in another work where full attribution is given.

© Derek Leman, 2006

Scripture quotations taken from the New American Standard Bible®, Copyright © 1960, 1962, 1963, 1968, 1971, 1972, 1973, 1975, 1977, 1995 by The Lockman Foundation.
Used by permission. (*www.Lockman.org*).
ISBN 0-9747814-3-6 Softcover

First printing 2006.

Library of Congress Control Number: 2006932667

This book is printed on archival quality paper.

Contents

About the Author

Derek Leman and his wife Linda have seven children and live in Snellville, Georgia. Derek is the Spiritual Leader of Tikvat David Messianic Congregation in Sandy Springs, Georgia.

Derek is the author of five books prior to *A New Look at the Old Testament*: *Paul Didn't Eat Pork, Jesus Didn't Have Blue Eyes, Proverbial Wisdom and Common Sense*, a daily devotional guide to the book of Proverbs, *Walking With Yeshua*, a guide for new believers, and *The Y'shua Challenge Part 2*, a four-unit discussion guide for sharing the good news of Messiah with an interested Jewish friend.

Derek is available to speak to churches and other groups. He can be contacted through the website *mtolivepress.com*.

To purchase more copies of this book or any other from Mt. Olive Press, go to *mtolivepress.com* or write to:

Mt. Olive Press
P.O. Box 659
Stone Mountain, GA 30086

Refer to the Quick Order Form at the back of this book.

A Roadmap to This Book

This book is intended as a roadmap for you in your own study of the Hebrew Bible, or as it is commonly known, the Old Testament. This introduction is a sort of roadmap to the roadmap so you will know what to expect from *A New Look at the Old Testament*.

I will use common terminology in this book, such as the term Old Testament, though I personally am more comfortable calling it the Hebrew Bible. It is not old or outdated. It is very much alive and a living revelation of God's character and will.

Whatever you may call it, the Old Testament makes up 80% of the English Bible. Isn't it time we learned how to read it, live it, appreciate it? This book is intended to help you do just that.

Why *A New Look at the Old Testament* is New

First, this is a different kind of book about the Old Testament. There are many excellent surveys of the Old Testament as well as commentaries. This book is an introduction to the ideas of the Old Testament to aid you in your own reading. It follows the order of the English Bible to make it easy for you to use this book to inform your own reading.

Second, this book is informed by a Messianic Jewish approach to scripture. It is not that a Messianic Jewish approach follows a different set of rules of interpretation, but there is a difference in approach. As part of the Jewish community, Messianic Judaism reads the Old Testament from the inside. Often Christian readings are looking back on a Jewish book as non-Jews. We in Messianic Judaism live the Old Testament. An interpretation in Leviticus is not mere historical interest to us, but affects how we live.

Third, this book will present some "new" ways of looking at Old Testament institutions and ideas. They are not really new in the sense of original, but they are "new" for a non-academic audience. For example, I will argue that the sacrifices of Israel did not bring forgiveness to the worshipper. This is not the usual interpretation but is discussed in academic commentaries such as that of Jacob Milgrom on Leviticus.

How to Use This Book

This book will be incomplete unless you read and benefit from the Old Testament. My intention is to help you better understand what you are reading, clear up some misconceptions, and get you reading and learning.

I recommend that you read *A New Look at the Old Testament* once for an overview and then begin a reading plan in the Old Testament. In "Appendix B" I suggest various reading plans for the Old Testament. Then, as you are reading the Old Testament, refer back to this book and compare notes.

So pick up your pen. Underline. Make notes. Get ready to grab your Bible and maybe a notebook. Plan to spend a year in reading the Old Testament.

Etz Khayim: A Tree of Life

Proverbs 3 describes God's Wisdom as a woman personified. Verse 18 says of Wisdom: "She is a tree of life to those who take hold of her, and happy are all who hold her fast."

In the Jewish worship service, when the scroll containing the words of Moses is put away, the people sing Proverbs 3:18. We are singing about the Bible. The Bible is a Tree of Life.

The Tree of Life is what the first man and woman lost in the Garden. God has given it back to us in the Bible. These are the words of life. They show us life and they point us to the only one who can give life. So take hold and be happy.

Chapter One

Unexpected Mentors and Surprising Beauty

The Old Testament is not a dead book. I found that out sitting in a Bible College classroom. Determined to learn about Judaism and Jewish culture, I decided that concentrating on the Old Testament would be wise.

I had limited knowledge of the Bible and the faith at the time. I had only become a follower of Jesus a year and a half before. My limited church experience taught me that the height of the Bible was Paul. Slightly below Paul in importance were the other letter writers such as Peter and John. Next were the gospels, then Genesis, and the Psalms, and perhaps Proverbs.

Definitely at the bottom of the ladder were the rest of the books—the rest of the Old Testament.

An Unexpected Mentor

My professor had glasses and a mustache, fitting perfectly with the stereotyped idea I had of an academic. The brown shirt and tie also seemed to fit. Combining these evidences with the chalk dust on his earth brown corduroy sport coat, I was confident he would be a brainy and, hopefully, interesting teacher.

Dr. John Walton did not disappoint. Immediately I could see that he was intense and emotional about the subject. That wouldn't have surprised me if, say, we were in a poetry class. But this was the Old Testament.

The class was on Wisdom Literature. I was so new to the faith I hadn't even read all of Job or any of Song of Songs. Proverbs and Psalms were somewhat familiar. Ecclesiastes definitely confused me.

There were times in that class when Dr. Walton would develop a theme from our readings that was intense and gripping. I had no idea that Job could be so riveting. The key to understanding Job was a triangle, Dr. Walton told us. At the top of the triangle is the idea that God is just. In one of the other corners of the triangle is the idea that Job was a righteous man. The last corner held the idea that God prospers the righteous and causes the wicked to suffer.

The friends of Job argued that Job had to have committed a sin in order to explain his tragedy. Job angrily denied their claim. The reader was privileged to know Job was right about that. No sin of Job caused the tragedy. Instead, Job eventually questioned the edges of the idea of God's justice.

What no one in the story considered was the third option, the one the writer was pointing to: that God prospers the righteous and makes the wicked suffer. While generally and ultimately true, this proposition is not universally true. In fact, the righteous often suffer and the wicked often prosper.

I don't remember Dr. Walton's exact words, but he began to talk about suffering and the confusion it causes believers. Trusting in God we often are hurt by suffering because we expect God to shield us from it. I remember seeing Dr. Walton's eyes water as he spoke. The words seemed real. He wasn't preaching or lecturing. He was talking with honesty about a mystery.

Then I sensed that the whole class was on the edge of crying. No one made a sound. The stillness was sharp. We were being deeply moved by the Old Testament. Its message was every bit as relevant today as any word from the New Testament. Paul's letters did not exceed Job in depth of human emotion or applicability of principle.

I was hooked. I took every class in Old Testament and with Dr. Walton that I could justify on my transcript.

Wrong Ideas and True Insights

The Old Testament occupies about 800 pages in one of the Bibles I keep on my desk. The New Testament makes up the last 224 pages of the 1,024 page edition. That makes the Old Testament in English about 80% of the Bible.

Assuming that the Bible is God's revelation of himself to humankind and that all of our English Bible belongs in God's revelation equally, most of what God has to say to us is in the Old Testament.

Yet the Old Testament gets the least attention, word for word, of any part of the Bible. I have observed many Christian settings in various denominations and churches. It would be considered unusually high for the Old Testament to make up 50% of the teaching and preaching in most churches. A number far below that is more common.

The 20% of the Bible called the New Testament gets 80% of the attention. There are many reasons why. Here are a few things people believe about the Old Testament which I would argue are wrong:

1. It is not as relevant to our modern situation because it was before the cross.
2. It is boring and too difficult to understand.
3. God is usually mad in the Old Testament and not very pleasant compared to God in the New Testament.
4. The commandments in the Old Testament are burdensome because God designed them to show Israel they could not keep the law.
5. It was written mostly to prepare the way for the New Testament and the Messiah, so it has for the most part been replaced by the better testament.
6. It is the Word of God because it shows the history of God's dealings with man, but for the most part its rules are outdated.

No wonder the Old Testament is not high on the reading list for most followers of Jesus. It seems about as likely to impact the life of a believer as reading the dictionary.

Here are some surprising truths about the Old Testament that should get any follower of Jesus excited about reading it:

1. Almost every truth of the New Testament was already present in the Old Testament. Very little is new in the New Testament.
2. The Old Testament has information about God's attributes in much greater detail than the New Testament.
3. The Old Testament was the book of Jesus and the apostles. They spoke about it constantly and memorized large portions of it. When they spoke of the necessity of knowing the Bible, they were referring to the Old Testament.
4. The Old Testament is filled with statements about God's favor for the undeserving (grace) and upholds love as the highest standard.
5. The Old Testament has more to say about prayer and worship than the New Testament.
6. The New Testament writers assume a thorough knowledge of the Old Testament. Lack of Old Testament knowledge is the greatest reason people fail to understand the New Testament properly.

Some of the statements above may seem hard to believe. That is why this book is here. Perhaps by the end you will agree with these claims about the Old Testament. It is a book about a magnificent and indescribably holy God who is worthy of worship that is joyous, extravagant, and large. It is a book of stories, predictions, wisdom, and prayers. It is a book that will change your life.

The Promise of Reading the Old Testament

Every part of the Old Testament is good reading. Every part is about who God is and how God wants us to live.

To be sure, some parts contain details which can be boring

to read. Long genealogies, lists, and poetic discourses can sometimes bring a snore. Some verses don't make for the best devotional reading. But that doesn't change the fact that every part of
the Old Testament is inspired by God and profitable.

The books of Moses, the Torah, are the foundation of all the
rest of the Bible. Creation, the fall of the world, the covenants
with Abraham and Israel, the commandments of God, and the
teachings of sacrifice and worship in the tabernacle are all the
beginnings of everything we believe. Contrary to most people's
instincts, books like Genesis and Leviticus are the most important
books to learn. That is why we will spend a great deal of time in
the Torah, from Creation to the Law.

The Torah will be much more devotional and filled with
insight than many people would imagine. They give a picture of
worship that is grand, awe-inspiring. They give a picture of faith
that is real, based on promises, and that carries over the centuries
and millennia. They show a way of life that is filled with justice,
love for neighbor, and love for God.

The Historical Books are also packed with meaning. There
are many characters, like Joshua, Samuel, David, Elijah, and
Nehemiah. Yet, often overlooked, is the main character, God. In
Joshua he is the warrior king conquering territory for his chosen
nation. In Samuel and Kings, he is the King above lesser kings,
the one judging and blessing based on their faithfulness or faith-
lessness. In Ezra and Nehemiah, he is the King receiving back his
people, and restoring Jerusalem. In Esther, God is not named, but
is the obvious source of salvation for the Jewish people threatened
by enemies.

The character of God in the historical books of the Bible is
clearly active and powerful in the world. We get an exclusive
God's-eye view of the working of two nations: Israel and Judah.
We see that God judges sin and yet has mercy on any who turn
even a little to him. This is the same God whom Jesus called
Father, forgiving yet justly opposed to sin and corruption.

In Chronicles, the history combines with poetry, as we see a focus on the revival of the people's faith and the beauty of the God-ordained temple worship. In Chronicles we see details of the choirs of Levites and temple ceremonies. A picture of grand, majestic worship emerges amidst the mixed history of Judah's kings.

The stories of the historical books are sometimes confusing and challenging, as in the last chapter of Judges, but most often memorable and inspiring. In this book, I will show that these stories are not parables or allegories, but real people experiencing God. Rather than trying to see them as types of Messiah we should see examples of God working in the lives of people. We may find here much hope for our own lives and God's working in us.

The poetic and wisdom books are a special joy for followers of Jesus. Many times when the Bible is abridged into merely a New Testament, the Psalms and Proverbs are attached. This is because next to the New Testament, these are the most read books in the Bible.

The Psalms are the prayers of Israel and the worship songs from the temple. We should read them as ancient hymns and prayers and imagine ourselves caught up in the worship with the people. When David says in Psalm 122:1, "I was glad when they said to me, 'Let us go to the house of the Lord,'" we should imagine the joy of worshipping with a group of devoted lovers of God.

The Proverbs are the pithy wisdom of Israel, mostly from Solomon. We should not make the mistake of turning them into promises. Righteous people do suffer. But it remains true that those who follow God lead better lives, if for no other reason than the fact that God matters more than possessions. Relationships and life skills will improve for those who make a habit of reading Proverbs.

Job and Ecclesiastes are harder books. They deal with the unanswered questions of wisdom. What about suffering? How is death fair? Doesn't God owe the righteous a good life? Both books take patience and were written for audiences who had time to read and think. For those patient enough to digest them, these literary masterpieces will affect the quality of everyday life.

Finally, the poetry of Song of Solomon is there to inspire us concerning romantic love while warning us of its perils. Many try to make the Song into a parable or allegory, but it is really a collection of love poems surrounding a proverb about love's power, peril, and promise in chapter 8.

Then the prophetic books round out the teaching and power of the Old Testament. Israel's prophets left us a mighty legacy, much of which remains to be fulfilled. Those who read the prophets regularly keep their eyes on Jerusalem, awaiting God's unfinished promises to Israel and the world.

The prophets speak in four ways: judgment, indictment, teaching, and promise. The judgments are hard for a reader to take, because we do not like to see pain. Yet they remind us that God does not take sin lightly. The indictments can also hurt, yet they often surprise us by showing God's priority on justice and kindness. A kind of righteousness that is obtainable and real can be seen in the prophets. The teaching passages are less common and all the more precious for that reason. In these God tells us directly what he wants from us: kindness and obedience to his commandments. Finally, and most gloriously, are the many promises of God in the prophets. Some have already come to pass, but many still await fulfillment. God will make all things new, starting from Jerusalem.

In this brief summary, you can see how promising the Old Testament is. Why wouldn't someone want to read worship, wisdom, real stories about God at work, and promises that give us great hope for the future? For the most part it is simply lack of knowledge that keeps people away from the Old Testament. Keep reading and see how your life is changed.

Chapter Two

Creation and Fall

The book of Genesis is special. In Hebrew, the first sentence has seven words, *Bereshit bara Elohim et ha-shamayim v'et ha-aretz*. In the beginning, God created the heavens and the earth.

Many people don't know that the verse numbers and chapter numbers of the Bible were added fairly recently. Sometimes, a good reader can see places where the chapters are divided poorly. Genesis chapter one is an example. It would be better if we regarded Genesis 1:1-2:3 as the first chapter.

The number seven keeps popping up in Genesis 1.[1] After the opening verse, which is an introduction, there are seven paragraphs:

Verses	Ending
1:2-5	"there was evening and there was morning, one day."
1:6-8	". . . a second day."
1:9-13	". . . a third day."
1:14-19	". . . a fourth day."
1:20-23	". . . a fifth day."
1:24-31	". . . the sixth day."
2:1-3	"Then God blessed the seventh day and sanctified it, because in it he had rested from all his work which God had created and made."

Just like the first sentence of Genesis has seven words, so also the seventh and last paragraph is special. It has three consecutive sentences of seven words each. The middle words of these three sentences are "the seventh day."

That is not all the sevens in Genesis one. Consider that the Hebrew words for God, heavens, and earth are all used in multiples of seven (35, 21, and 21 times respectively).

The words light and day are used a total of seven times in paragraph one and light is used seven times in paragraph four. Water is used seven times in paragraphs two and three. Genesis 1:2 has fourteen words in Hebrew—exactly.

As if that wasn't enough, in Genesis 1-4, the word God is used a total of 70 times.

The Creation Message

It seems that something very special is going on in Genesis. Moses has left is a carefully written account, even down to poetic tricks with the number seven.

The number seven has a lot more significance than most people realize.

The moon takes 29 1/2 days to revolve around the earth. The earth takes 365 1/4 days to revolve around the earth. The number seven does not divide evenly into either of these numbers.

Yet the whole world has a seven-day week. Where did it come from? It came from Genesis one. The Jews spread the Torah and the seven-day week to the Christian world. The Christians spread it to the Roman world. Through the Roman world, the seven-day week became the world's calendar.

The seven-day week, followed by Christians and Jews as well as Buddhists, atheists, Hindus, Muslims, animists, and everyone in the world, is a symbol of creation. Many in the world disbelieve in the Bible's account of creation, yet follow the Bible's seven-day week. Just as the seven-day week lies at the heart of human civilization, so does creation—even for those who do not believe in it.

God's hand in creation is one-half of the reason we are the way we are. The other half is the fall.

Creation in Moses' Time

The Babylonian creation account, which is thought to be at least as old as Abraham,[2] gives a very different picture of creation:

> *Then the Lord paused to view her dead body,*
> *That he might divide the monster and do artful works.*
> *He split her like a shellfish into two parts:*
> *Half of her he set up and ceiled it as Sky.*[3]

This is the story of Marduk, chief god of Babylon. Marduk is a storm god and corresponds in numerous ways to Zeus in Greek mythology and Baal in Canaanite mythology.

Marduk made a deal with the other gods. He would rule over them as king if he could kill Tiamat, the dragon of chaos, representing the saltwater oceans. Tiamat was a much older goddess than Marduk and killing her would not be easy.

Nonetheless, when Marduk did kill her, he cut her in half. One half of her body became earth and the other half sky. He later slew her husband, Kingu, and made humankind from a mixture of clay and the blood of the god Kingu.

The people in Moses' day had similar thoughts about creation even in different areas where the mythology varied, such as in Egypt. What mattered most to the ancient mind was not existence, but order. How do you explain the separation of seas and clouds, water and land? How did the cycle of sun and moon begin?

To the pagans, this was the magic of gods and goddesses. Marduk, for example, took the tablets of destinies from Tiamat and Kingu. With these tablets, Marduk was able to assign a place for everything: kinds of plants and animals, cycles of sun and moon, seasons of the earth, and so on.

The modern reader of Genesis one may wonder why it focuses more on order than existence. God separates night from day, land from water, and cloud from ocean. God makes animals and plants by separate kinds which cannot intermix.

Genesis is showing us something fundamental about God,

about our world, and about us. In the words of Italian Jewish scholar, Umberto Cassuto:

> The purpose of the Torah in this section is to teach us that the whole world and all that it contains were created by the word of the One God, according to His will, which operates without restraint.[4]

God is the reason we have a seven-day week in all the countries of the world. God is also the reason animal and plant kinds are separate and unmixable. God is also the reason why we are the way we are.

Created in God's Image

Everything else God made he spoke into being. But people were created differently. We were formed, sculpted you might say, from the clay of the ground.[5] We are his masterpiece, the height of all creation. The stars are beautiful and the oceans mighty, but God merely spoke them into being. The importance of humankind is much greater. We were shaped by his hand like a work of art.

We are also, Genesis says, made in his image. When a couple has a son or daughter, the child has the eyes, hair, and natural personality traits such as shyness or daring of the parents. Children are made in the image of their parents.

So it is with us and God. Why do you think we write so many books? God's power is in the spoken and written word. So humankind uses language like no other creature on earth. We are children of our Father.

Why do you think we make so many roads, buildings, and cities? Why do we make works of art? Why do we invent? Our Father is a creator and so are we.

Why do we love others? Evolutionary theory cannot explain love. Sometimes love works against survival, as when a person risks life for a stranger. Love is one of the maker's marks we bear, like a painter's signature on a canvas.

Genesis is a book that explains why we are the way we are.

The Fall

Yet love, creativity, and the use of language are not all there is to humanity. Sadly there are wars, mob violence, genocide, sadistic torture, deceit, manipulation, and a thousand other evils in humankind.

A human being seems to be a contradiction of love and hate, goodness and evil. In a way, we have two sides: the image of God and something else, a fallen, evil nature.

Genesis explains that too. Ancient man was concerned about death, suffering, and evil. It is not new to history for people to think about these things. Such themes are in the ancient myth of Gilgamesh, a story predating Abraham.

Gilgamesh, the ancient Sumerian hero, was depressed by the death of his friend Enkidu. Experiencing death so closely, the powerful king decided to find out how to conquer death. He met an immortal man named Utnapisti who told him about a plant at the bottom of the sea that rejuvenated youth. Gilgamesh found the plant, but left it on the shore while taking a swim. A serpent stole his immortality away while he was swimming.[6]

The ancients wanted to know where death came from. Remarkably, in the widespread myth of Gilgamesh we see a remarkable correspondence to the Bible: a serpent was responsible for death.

The Genesis account tells us how it really happened. The Bible account also involves a serpent.

God placed the man and later the woman in the Garden he had made for them. They were immortal and perfect. No evil was on the earth.

God gave them a choice, a fundamental choice between knowledge and life. The man and woman chose knowledge after a serpent deceived the woman and created doubts about God.

Because the man and woman chose knowledge over life, chose to disobey God's instructions to prefer life to knowledge, God sentenced us to death, "For you are dust, and to dust you shall return."[7]

After that, we were banished from the Garden and we lost immortality. We also knew our nakedness, because now we had knowledge of good and evil.

Before the fall of humankind from the Garden, we were innocent. God's original plan is not detailed in Genesis because we did not follow it. One can speculate, however, that if we had eaten only from the Tree of Life, and the other permissible trees, we would still be immortal. And God would have given us knowledge of good and evil in the proper time, when he could show us how to be good and not evil.

But we chose knowledge and with it came death and evil. The world itself became cursed. Typhoons and lightning, wars and plagues characterize our world today.

And how far people have fallen! Depravity is the norm, not the exception. A rosy view of humanity is easily shattered by watching the evening news. Adults molest children. Tribes and ethnic groups seek to kill whole peoples. Even so-called normal people exhibit evil and death in their lives—betraying spouses, rejecting loved ones, and centering their lives on themselves.

Genesis and the Cross

Genesis is Torah. Torah means "teaching." Genesis is the first book of Moses, the first book of the Torah.

Far from dry, impractical, and outdated, as some people imagine the Torah to be, Genesis gets to the heart of who we are, why we are here, and what our condition is.

We are children of a Father who made us for glory and goodness. We are like him, and this is why goodness and love are still the human ideal and still exist in the lives of people.

We are also, sadly, children of the fall. We bear in us the knowledge of good and evil without the ability to avoid evil and choose only good. We did not follow God's plan and so we are unprepared for life, especially for the unending life God has planned for us.

Genesis is best understood by those who know the difference

between the first Adam and the last Adam. Paul tells us the first Adam is the one who brought us down into death and sin.[8] Adam chose knowledge over life. Jesus chose obedience over life.

Genesis shows us the need for a second Adam. In fact, many would see in Genesis hints of the cross.

The man and woman knew their nakedness when they discovered the knowledge of good and evil. Their nakedness was more than a lack of clothes. It represented for them a new knowledge of sexual sin. They sought to cover it with fig leaves, but God made them coats of skin.[9]

There had been no death in the Garden. Yet for an animal to give up its skin, death is required. Perhaps we are supposed to see that the first sacrifice was made by God for Adam and Eve.

Later, Abel offers to God sacrifices of animals as does Noah.[10] Then, in the story of Abraham and his son Isaac, we see clearly the death of an animal in place of the death of a person.[11]

Those who accept the New Testament can see the cross in the Old. Genesis reveals how we got to the place where a cross is needed. The sacrifice of Jesus answers the question: how can a people who chose knowledge return to life?

Chapter Three
Covenant Faith

A braham was a pagan living in Mesopotamia amongst other pagans. It sounds odd to a modern reader to hear such a statement about Abraham, the father of faith. Yet at the feast of First-Fruits the Israelites were required to say to the priest, "My father was a wandering Aramean."[1] Abraham was of a pagan people, the Arameans (or Syrians).

Abraham, originally called Abram, had no more concept of the true God than any pagan in Babylon, Hatti, or Egypt. Idolatry was part of the way of Abraham's family and shows up even generations later. When Rachel, married to Abraham's grandson, fled Laban, she brought with her the household idol for luck.[2] Can there be any doubt that Abraham himself grew up with idolatrous practices and beliefs?

One day something extraordinary happened to Abraham. He heard the voice of a god saying:

> Go forth from your country, and from your relatives and from your father's house, to the land which I will show you; and I will make you a great nation, and I will bless you, and make your name great; and so you shall be a blessing; and I will bless those who bless you, and the one who curses you I will curse. And in you all the families of the earth will be blessed.[3]

We have no idea if Abraham knew who the Lord was before this or if the Lord introduced himself before telling this to Abraham. What we do know is that Abraham took this word from God very seriously.

He left his family, except his nephew Lot, and went to

Canaan. He thereafter regarded God as his only God. He may not have considered him the only God in existence, but at least he would be the only God Abraham would worship.

Abraham passed it down to Isaac, who passed it down to Jacob, who passed it down to the fathers of the twelve tribes: God is the Lord and he alone is to be served.

The One-Sided Covenant

All God asked Abraham to do was leave his family and the place his family dwelt. This might seem a difficult thing. It was not.

Abraham was from a nomadic people. Much as the nomadic sheepherders today in the Middle East, it was common to move around with the seasons and even migrate at times to find better land.

Abraham's family, led by his father Terah, had already made a long journey from Ur of the Chaldeans to Haran on their way to Canaan.[4] There is some debate about which Ur is meant, a large, well-known city in the south of Babylon or a lesser known city north and east of Israel. The location of Haran is fairly certain. Abraham's family had already been on its way to Canaan when God called on Abraham. So moving from his place would be an easy and natural thing for this Aramean to do.

As for Abraham separating from his father, while this may have been hard to do emotionally, nomadic people like Abraham expected to separate at times. Abraham was a wealthy man with many animals. He and his father would have had to separate anyway, most likely, because of the size of their flocks and herds.

So God promised Abraham the world simply for going to a land he was already headed toward. God said he would bless Abraham, asking only that he separate himself, as nomads are already prone to do. It was a one-sided covenant.

The old stories of the Ancient Near East contain tales of gods and goddesses talking with humans. Yet Abraham's experience was unique. This God not only spoke with him, but also made a covenant with him. And more than that, the covenant had nothing in it for the God who made it. It was not divine manipulation, as was common in pagan myths, but divine gift, pure and free. Who ever heard of a god like this?

Covenants had long been a part of Ancient Near Eastern life. Neighboring peoples made covenants over things like water rights.[5] Powerful rulers made covenants with lesser rulers, always to their benefit.

Yet this God made a covenant with Abraham that was all to Abraham's benefit. And a covenant was binding. Abraham knew he was in for blessing.

There has always been a ceremony to ratify a covenant. Even today when lawyers and clients sit across a conference table and sign thick stacks of papers, we know a covenant is being made. And there is always a consequence for breaking a covenant—monetary or judicial.

God's ceremony to ratify his covenant with Abraham came in Genesis 15. Abraham was put to sleep and he saw a blazing oven floating through the air, a symbol of fire and divine power that would have made sense to Abraham. On the ground there were cut up animals. The floating, flaming oven went between the pieces of slaughtered animals. Abraham did nothing in the ceremony but watch.

The meaning of the ceremony was clear, and parallels exist in the Ancient Near East.[6] Usually both parties in a covenant would walk between the animal pieces. The message of this action was simple: "May I be cut into pieces like these animals if I fail to keep this covenant."

In Abraham's case, God walked between the pieces. God was saying, "If I fail to bless you as I promised, then may I be killed and cut into pieces."

Abraham did not walk through the pieces. This was a one-sided covenant. It was all God, and Abraham simply had to believe and receive.

There is a theological word for something like this. We call it grace. In simple terms it means divine favor, a favor that is undeserved. Abraham did not merit this covenant. He received it as a gift from the God who gives blessings out of pure love.

The Covenant Promise

Abraham was already seventy-five years old when he came to Canaan.[7] He was far too old to have children, at least by Sarah, who was only ten years younger.[8]

Yet God's first promise to Abraham was, "I will make you a great nation." This childless nomad hardly seemed a candidate to start a great nation of people.

Ancient people thought a great deal about their progeny. Who would live after them? Would their family name be great? This was more to be desired than any level of wealth. If a wealthy and powerful man's line was cut off, it was all for nothing.

God's promise to Abraham was exactly what a man of his time would consider the greatest blessing. Even Abraham, though, had no idea how God's word would come to pass. From Abraham came the people Israel, the Jewish people, the Chosen People. The world has been shaped and changed more by this one small people—today there are only 15 million Jews worldwide—than any other people in history.

God promised second of all, "I will bless you, and make your name great." Not many people from 2000 B.C.E. are known today. Abraham is a name known by billions of people.

Third, God promised, "You shall be a blessing." This verse can be taken two ways. It might simply mean, "Other people will use your name as a blessing." People might say, "May you be as blessed as Abraham." Yet it also might mean more. Perhaps God was saying, "You, Abraham, will be a channel through which I will bring blessing to the world."

Fourth, God promised to do more than simply bless Abraham. Other peoples, leaders, and nations would receive either blessing or curse from God based on how they treated Abraham's family. Abimelech, an early king in the region of the Philistines, experienced this firsthand—twice. First he unwittingly tried to take Sarah into his harem. God told him in a dream he was a dead man, for Abraham was his prophet.[9] Later, Abimelech, or more likely his son, had a dispute with Isaac over water rights. Abimelech saw that God was blessing Isaac and he was afraid. He made a covenant of peace with Isaac out of fear of the Lord.[10]

God blesses those who love Israel and the Jewish people. He curses nations and leaders who oppose the Jewish people. It is a principle going back 4,000 years in God's plan.

Finally, God said, "In you all the families of the earth will be blessed." As with the third promise, and even more so based on the Hebrew grammar, this statement could mean either that Abraham's name would be used in blessings or that he would be a channel of God's blessing to the world.

Abraham's family certainly has been a blessing to the world. Through Abraham's descendants we received the knowledge of God, the scriptures, and Messiah. The land which God called Abraham to is the land in which Jesus lived and died and rose again. It is the land to which he will return. It is the land in which we will worship God in the Age to Come. It is the land in which God's city, the New Jerusalem will come down.

Truly all the families of the earth have been blessed through Abraham.

Faith Like Abraham

Abraham did not have to do something difficult for God. He did not have to earn his way with God. In fact, God said:

> *Then he [Abraham] believed in the Lord; and He [the Lord] reckoned it to him as righteousness.*[11]

God credited righteousness to Abraham because of his faith. There is a theological word for this also: grace, undeserved favor.

Abraham's faith in God was very real and living. He did not believe some religious dogma or participate in some existing religious system. In fact, Abraham made altars to God and offered sacrifices on them.[12] He called on the name of the Lord, a way of describing prayer.[13] Abraham knew God, loved him, and served him in any way he could. That was his faith.

Abraham talked to God and listened to God. When God told him to do something, he did it. Once, having met a priest of God Most High, who Abraham saw as one and the same as the Lord, Abraham gave away ten percent of all the spoils of battle to God.[14] When God said that Abraham should circumcise himself and his family, he did it.[15] When God asked Abraham to give up his only son, Abraham was ready to do it also. His faith was that deep.

Sacrificial Faith

Human sacrifice—the concept was not as out of the question for ancients as it is for moderns. The thing about the human sinful nature is that it conforms to social norms. If society accepts the concept of human sacrifice, even marginally, there will be people who will consider it.

In Abraham's case, God commanded it. He said, "Take now your son, your only son, whom you love, Isaac, and go to the land of Moriah, and offer him there as a burnt offering on one of the mountains of which I will tell you."[16]

Abraham had no way to know God would not let him go through with it. There is evidence of human sacrifice in North Africa and the Ancient Near East. Archaeologists have found children's tombs with evidence that they had been sacrificed in Carthage and as close to Israel as Cyprus.[17] The Bible mentions that kings like Ahaz and Manasseh sacrificed some of their children.[18] In Jerusalem, the Valley of Hinnom is called Ge-Hinnom in Hebrew, from which the word Gehenna is derived, a term used comparatively with hell in the New Testament. It was the place where children were sacrificed in Israel. Josiah, the reforming king, destroyed the place there, called the Tophet, so that people could not continue sacrificing children.[19]

Most of these examples are much later than the time of Abraham, but the practice almost certainly was known in his day as well. In the Torah, God forbade child sacrifice: "Any man from the sons of Israel or from the aliens sojourning in Israel who gives any of his offspring to Molech, shall surely be put to death."[20]

Abraham expected this God who had led him to Canaan and had been his friend for years really wanted him to sacrifice his son. And Abraham was willing to do it.

As difficult as human sacrifice would be, for Abraham there was another issue entirely: the covenant promise. For a man in Abraham's culture, having a successful line of descendants was more important than all the wealth in the world. God had promised a great nation would come through him.

Abraham was seventy-five when God made the promise to him.[21] By the time he and Sarah had their child, Isaac, Abraham was one-hundred years old when Isaac was born.[22] he had waited for twenty-five years for God to keep his promise! How long can a person keep believing in a promise when God does not bring it to pass? How old would a person have to be to finally decide God would not give them a child?

Throughout the story of Abraham's life, the covenant promise of God is continually threatened. Many times Abraham's own actions threatened to keep the covenant from coming to pass. Sarah was in danger at times and Abraham would have no wife to bring him a child. Abraham nearly gave the Promised Land away to Lot in a foolish gesture of courtesy. The Abraham story revolved around the threat to the covenant as the following table shows:[23]

12:10-20	Covenant Threat #1: Sarah Almost Taken
13:1-13	Covenant Threat #2: Abram Nearly Gives the Land to Lot
13:14-18	God Reiterates the Promise of the Land
14:1-16	Covenant Threat #3: Abram Almost Killed Rescuing Lot
14:17-24	Interlude: Abram, Melchizedek, and Faithfulness to God

15:1-4	Covenant Threat #4: Abram Wants to Name Eliezer His Heir
15:5-21	Covenant Reiterated and Formally Cut
16:1-16	Covenant Threat #5: Abram Seeks an Heir Through Hagar
17:1-16	Covenant Reiterated: New Names and a Sign (Circumcision)
17:17-22	Covenant Threat #6: Abraham Offers Ishmael as Heir

Yet for all the times Abraham nearly lost God's promise to inherit the land and father a great nation, no covenant threat comes close to the time God asked him to sacrifice Isaac.

He had waited twenty-five years to realize the promise in his extreme old age. Now Isaac was older and Abraham was past being old. Now after all this, after Abraham's faith over many years in an impossible promise, God says: give it all back.

Abraham faced a question that would haunt Job years later: do I love God for God or for the blessings he brings? If God took away all his blessings, would I still trust in him?

Amazingly, Abraham's faith was that strong. He was willing not only to sacrifice his child, but also to give up the promise God had made. Abraham would not father a great nation. Abraham would not be a blessing to the world. God and Sarah would be all this aged nomad would have left. And he was willing to do it.

What was God's purpose in this? People have speculated that:

1. God did this for Abraham's sake, to strengthen his faith.
2. God did this to show Abraham and Israel that child sacrifice is abominable.
3. God did this for Isaac's sake and for all of us, so that our faith would be strengthened.
4. God did this as a type of Messiah, God's only Son, whom God would sacrifice for us.

Yet the story itself answers the question. God's primary purpose can be seen at the end of the story. God substitutes, by divine providence, a ram whose horns are caught in the brush, for Isaac. Then God says, "Now I know that you fear God, since you have not withheld your son, your only son, from Me."[24] God wanted to test Abraham's faith, just as Genesis 22:1 says.[25]

"But wait," someone might object, "God knows everything and he knew if Abraham had faith or not." Sure, and most women know their husbands love them, so why bother arranging special time together for romance? Isn't it enough to just know? God wanted to see Abraham's faith in action because God loved Abraham and God desires to be loved in return. Abraham's faith pleased God just as our faith also pleases him.

Covenant Faith Today

Abraham believed in God's covenant promises. His covenant faith passed down to Isaac and Jacob and went into Egypt with Joseph to reemerge in Moses' time.

God reiterated his covenant promise to Isaac in Genesis 26:3-5:

> Sojourn in this land and I will be with you and bless you, for to you and to your descendants I will give all these lands, and I will establish the oath which I swore to your father Abraham. I will multiply your descendants as the stars of heaven, and will give your descendants all these lands; and by your descendants all the nations of the earth shall be blessed; because Abraham obeyed Me and kept My charge, My commandments, My statutes and My laws.

Later, Jacob would describe God as "the fear of Isaac," showing that Jacob was aware from childhood of his father's faith.[26]

Jacob's own story was more convoluted. For years he did not understand that God's blessing was with him. Through manipulation he tried to bring himself blessing. He traded for Esau's birthright and stole Esau's firstborn blessing. When he was with Laban, he resorted to magical superstition to try and win animals for his herds. God reiterated his blessings to Jacob many times, but Jacob did not understand and thought he had stumbled into God's house by chance. He couldn't grasp that God wanted to bless him through the promise to Abraham.

It wasn't until Jacob was in fear of his life, returning to the land where his brother was likely to want to kill him, that Jacob was humbled into realizing God would bless him. God sent an angel to meet him and wrestle with him and break him down.[27]

Finally Jacob realized it was true. God really was blessing the descendants of his grandfather, Abraham. Jacob really was the father of the tribes of Israel. The great nation God had promised was forming. Those who blessed the children of Abraham would be blessed and those who cursed them would be cursed.

Jacob learned what many need to know today. Israel remains God's people. Paul said, "God has not rejected his people, whom he foreknew."[28] It might seem that the majority of Israel's lack of faith in Jesus the Messiah forfeited their blessing. But Paul countered that idea by saying of Israel, "The gifts and the calling of God are irrevocable."[29] Those who love the Jewish people and Israel will be blessed and those who oppose Israel break themselves on the Rock of Ages.

Yet even Abraham himself did not know how true the covenant promises would become. God had said in Genesis 12:3: "In you all the families of the earth will be blessed." It was Paul, a Pharisee who loved Jesus, that the full meaning of this promise came to be known:

> The Scripture, foreseeing that God would justify the Gentiles by faith, preached the gospel beforehand to Abraham, saying, "All the nations will be blessed in you."[30]

The Hebrew word for "nations" also means Gentiles, or non-Jews. Through Abraham's seed the whole world was blessed.

Paul sees a mystical covenant promise here also, for the word seed is a collective plural. A collective plural looks the same when it refers to one thing or many things. So, for example, we use the word deer in English. Whether it is one deer or two hundred deer, we do not put an 's' on the end of the word.

So, that word seed in God's promise to Abraham has a mystical sense to it. The seed of Abraham are many: the Jewish people throughout all the ages. Yet seed is also singular. And there is one seed of Abraham through which the blessing came:

> Now the promises were spoken to Abraham and to his seed. He does not say, "And to seeds," as referring to many, but rather to one, "And to your seed," that is, Messiah.[31]

God promised Abraham more than he realized, even with his remarkable faith. God promised to bring Messiah through him, the seed of Abraham who would bless the world.

Like Abraham, we should see God as the covenant-blessing God. He keeps his promises in ways beyond our imagining. And his covenants are one-sided, full of undeserved favor for those who believe his promises.

Chapter Four

Bulls, Goats, and Worship

At the front of the auditorium, a grey-suited man in black wing-tip shoes comes to a wooden pulpit. In the background, a piano is playing. The sun is shining through colored windows in a room carpeted in red. The seats, church pews, are softly cushioned, also in red. The red carpet, the cushioned pews, and the dark-stained walls give the room a completely different feeling than an office or living room.

The congregation is dressed well for this Sunday service. The man in the grey suit, the music minister, asks everyone to turn to a certain page in a book of hymns. The congregation dutifully turns and begins singing as the music minister leads them. After a few hymns, everyone is asked to shake hands and welcome one another. Another hymn after that and four men come to the front of the auditorium. One of them intones a barely audible prayer, something about God's house and an offering.

Several plates are passed around and money is placed in them to support the church. A beautiful melody from the piano fills the auditorium as the people wait. Then a man in a blue suit comes to the pulpit. With a large, black, leather Bible in hand he speaks in three points, all beginning with the letter "p" from a Bible text.

After the message, the man in the blue suit waits at the front as the piano plays again. The grey-suited music minister leads the people softly in singing an inviting hymn. The people wait to see if anyone will come forward to publicly declare their faith, to join the church, or to request baptism. Most weeks no one comes.

So goes a worship service in many churches in America. The

ideas expressed in the songs and the sermons help the people to grow in their faith. The special atmosphere of the worship auditorium feels holy to the people attending. The special clothing of the ministers lends an air of officiality as does the piano music.

There are other styles. In some auditoriums, the speakers shout more and the people move more. In some, the speakers dress more stylishly or casually. Some worship centers look like theaters or even converted warehouses. Some pulpits are made of clear Lucite instead of wood. Some have brighter colors and look more modern. Still, there are recognizable styles and patterns to the dress, environment, and music. They all spell worship to the audiences attending.

If you ask many people how a modern church service compares to the worship of the Old Testament, included in their answers would be some variation of the following response: the worship in the church is more spiritual and theirs was more physical.

The interesting thing is that physical criteria largely affect what we consider to be worship. If a group of people simply met on a street corner, read from the Bible and sang some songs, many people would not consider it worship. In our own churches and congregations we have certain expectations of the physical environment, appropriate dress, and the cultural style of the music. Furthermore, our buildings have large mortgages or were purchased at the end of large fundraising campaigns. Our sound systems cost thousands or sometimes much more. Yet we imagine that our worship is more spiritual than physical.

Tabernacle Worship
In the days of King David, the tabernacle had been newly moved to Jerusalem. Pilgrims came from all over the land, from amongst all ten tribes. The longest journey was for the tribe of Dan, in far northern Israel. God did not demand weekly worship services, which is a good thing since some people had to walk more than a week just to arrive at them.

The pilgrims came three times a year: Passover, Weeks (Pentecost), and Tabernacles. If modern worship services are often characterized as three songs, a welcome, an offering, and a sermon, the ancient worship services of the Israelites could be summarized as follows:

1. The pilgrimage to Jerusalem, a worship experience in and of itself.
2. Approaching Jerusalem with Songs of Ascent and responsive psalms.
3. Staying in a home or camping around Jerusalem for the festival.
4. Eating festive meals from the sacrificial meat and the tithes of the produce of the land.
5. Standing with the throng in front of the gates to witness the ceremonies and participate with the crowd.
6. Drawing near to the tabernacle itself to bring animal and grain offerings to God.

Their worship was no more or less physical than modern worship and no less spiritual. In fact, in many cases their worship was more intense, their crowds larger, and their level of participation higher than in the modern church service.

The Pilgrimage and Songs of Ascent

Some of the people, to be sure, lived very close to Jerusalem and had a short journey to the tabernacle. Others might journey for a week or more to get there.

Moses said, "Three times in a year all your males shall appear before the Lord your God in the place which He chooses, at the Feast of Unleavened Bread and at the Feast of Weeks and at the Feast of Booths, and they shall not appear before the Lord empty-handed."[1]

Not everyone obeyed the commandment of God to come three times a year to the sanctuary of God. Archaeology has confirmed what the Bible says over and over: that many Israelites practiced idolatry and only partially obeyed God's instructions. Nonetheless, in the days of a king like David, who was committed to God's commandments, participation was no doubt quite high. Even in the dark times of kings like Ahab, there were still thousands who believed and obeyed God.[2]

Groups of families and entire villages would come together in caravans, with donkeys and carts bearing sacks of grain, dried fruits, flasks of wine, and jugs of pure olive oil for their tithes. Many would lead small flocks of goats and lambs for animal offerings to be made while in Jerusalem. Others would bring money and buy their sacrificial animals in the city.

It seems that the practice was to sing or chant the Psalms, in the original Hebrew, during the pilgrimage or at least when they neared Jerusalem. When climbing the hill of Jerusalem, a long ascent, the people sang special psalms called Songs of Ascent, Psalms 120-134. They sang things like:

> I was glad when they said to me, "Let us go to the house of the Lord. Our feet are standing within your gates, O Jerusalem, Jerusalem, that is built as a city that is compact together; to which the tribes go up, even the tribes of the Lord-- an ordinance for Israel-- to give thanks to the name of the Lord.[3]

As they came within sight of the temple, quite possibly some of the responsive psalms were used. Groups of pilgrims already gathered in a throng in front of the tabernacle gates would call out, "Give thanks to the Lord, for he is good." The approaching pilgrims would respond, "For his lovingkindness is everlasting."[4]

The worship at the sanctuary of God had not even begun, yet the atmosphere of worship and wonder was there. Just the journey itself was part of the worship of the God of Israel.

Dwelling and Feasting in Jerusalem

Passover and Tabernacles lasted for seven days. The Feast of

Weeks, named for the seven weeks between the Sabbath of Passover and the Feast of Weeks, lasted only a day.⁵ Nevertheless, some pilgrims arrived early and stayed late. Jerusalem and the surrounding hills turned into a festival campground for days and weeks, three times a year.

For Passover and Weeks, the people camped in tents or stayed as guests in homes. For Tabernacles, also called Booths, the people made booths with cut branches to live in for the entire week (or longer).

The people brought their tithes with them. The time of the year dictated what they might have with them, but grain, olive oil, wine, dried fruit, and meat for peace offerings were constantly available. It is a little known fact that the tithes were first eaten by the people, as Deuteronomy 14:23 says: "You shall eat in the presence of the Lord your God, at the place where He chooses to establish His name, the tithe of your grain, your new wine, your oil, and the firstborn of your herd and your flock, so that you may learn to fear the Lord your God always." The tithes were all shared, especially with Levites, priests, orphans, and widows, and the remainder that was uneaten was donated.

It is not easy to interpret the tithe laws today, since they are listed in several places and it is unclear how the different commands fit together. It is possible that there was only one tithe, eaten by the worshippers and the remainder donated to the sanctuary. It is also possible that there was a second and even a third tithe. Numbers 18 speaks of a tithe to the Levites, which may simply mean the remainder of the festival tithe or could be a second one. Deuteronomy 14:28 speaks of a tithe every third year which was to be stored within the towns for the poor, widows, and orphans.

Whatever the exact practice of tithing was, it is sure that the people had plenty to eat at the pilgrim feasts. At Passover they ate unleavened cakes of bread with wine, oil, and meat. At the other feasts, they ate without restrictions of their crops and the flocks and herds.

For the average person in biblical times, meat was a rare luxury. The festivals would be a time to eat like no other time of the year. Lambs and goats were eaten on the night of Passover. At other times, peace offerings were brought to the priests and most of the meat was for the people to eat at the feast. Worshipping God was not in any sense boring, but the greatest celebration of the year.

Worshipping with the Throng

Our era of church life is known for mega-churches. Churches with 2,000 or more weekly attenders are becoming more common. Churches with 10,000 or more attenders are not unheard of.

Yet the crowds at the sanctuary in Jerusalem numbered in the tens and hundreds of thousands.

A modern person looking at a model or picture of the tabernacle of Israel, or the later temple of Israel, tends to wonder where the people were supposed to stand or sit. Ancient temples, and Israel's was no exception, were not buildings for the congregation. They were places where the priests carried out worship to the gods and goddesses.

Israel's tabernacle and temple were not so dissimilar to the temples of other peoples. In the courtyard, there was an altar for animal sacrifices and a basin for the priests to ritually wash themselves. Near the back of the courtyard was a tent, in the temple a stone building, which housed more places for the priests to administer worship and in the very back was a room separated by a veil. Inside that room, the Most Holy Place or the Holy of Holies, God's presence dwelt in a physical manifestation.

The people did not congregate in the courtyard of the tabernacle—it wouldn't hold a very large crowd. They congregated in front of the tabernacle courtyard, at the gates. The throng of tens and perhaps hundreds of thousands would fill a vast area in front. There was no sermon. Who would hear it?

This is not to say that the people did not hear the reading of the scriptures, primarily Moses. Deuteronomy 24:8 refers to the

Levitical priests teaching the people. Doubtless this happened in smaller groups, at individual campsites.

Nor could everyone see what was going on at the tabernacle. Just to be near while the priests were ministering was awesome. Just to be close to God's presence inside the tabernacle was overwhelming. To see the smoke rising from the festival burnt offerings inspired worship and reverence. To participate in the crowd's chanting of psalms to God was a moving service of worship.

This is why David wrote, "I was glad when they said to me, "Let us go to the house of the Lord."[6] It is why David also said, "A day in Your courts is better than a thousand outside."[7]

The Worship of God with Sacrifices

The greatest worship moment in the life of an Israelite was bringing an offering to God. The offerer, man or woman, Israelite or Gentile, got to draw nearer to God at that moment than any other time.[8]

Leviticus 1:3 says, "He shall offer it at the doorway of the tent of meeting, that he may be accepted before the Lord." The tent of meeting is the name for the tent itself, inside the tabernacle courtyard. The offerer came in between the altar and the tent. In temple times they came between the altar and the temple building itself. They were only yards away from the tent into which only the priests could go and which had, in the back part, a room where the Ark of the Covenant and the presence of God dwelt in a physical manifestation of fire and cloud.

In short, bringing an animal sacrifice got you closer to God than any other thing you could do. This was your moment, to stand near to God's sanctuary, to be in the midst of his courtyard, to see his holy altar, and to be in the midst of the priests of God.

The sacrifices of Israel are much misunderstood and maligned. The following chart addresses the most common misconceptions:

Myths About the Sacrifices	The Truth About the Sacrifices
Every time you sin, you have to offer a sacrifice.	Sacrifices for the sins of the entire nation were offered twice a day. Individuals mostly brought sacrifices only at the three annual pilgrim festivals.
Women and Gentiles could not directly bring their sacrifices to God, but were restricted to areas outside the tabernacle.	Women and Gentiles were not restricted, but brought their sacrifices just like Israelite men.
The priest slaughtered your animal, cut it up, and offered the blood on the altar.	You slaughtered your own animal and cut it up. The priests caught the blood and dashed it against the altar.
The sacrifices were cruel and bloodthirsty.	Unless you are a vegetarian, your meat-eating leads to the same kind of animal slaughtering. Modern animal slaughtering is actually more cruel, with mass production outweighing consideration of the animals.
The sacrifices were a primitive way to worship God.	The sacrifices were an awe-inspiring way to worship God, bringing you closer to God than any other activity.
The sacrifices are a thing of the past, never to return. They have been replaced and surpassed by the sacrifice of Jesus.	The sacrifices are part of our future. Paul offered sacrifices in his day (Acts 21:26). The temple will be rebuilt and sacrifices will again be offered in the days of Jesus' kingdom (Ezek. 40:39). The sacrifices at the temple serve a different purpose than the cross.
The sacrifices brought forgiveness to the offerer.	The sacrifices kept the sanctuary clean so God could dwell there.

To better understand the sacrifices of Israel, we need to understand some basic concepts:

1. God's presence dwelling in Israel's midst.
2. The concept of pollution, impurity, and defilement.
3. The cleansing function of the sacrifices.
4. The types of sacrifices and their purpose.

God's Presence in the Midst of Israel

When Israel was leaving Egypt, being chased by Pharaoh's army, God's presence began traveling with them in a pillar of cloud. Many people think that in the daytime his presence was a cloud and at night it turned into fire. Actually, the words of Exodus 40:38 make the phenomenon of God's presence clear:

> For throughout all their journeys, the cloud of the Lord was on the tabernacle by day, and there was fire in it by night, in the sight of all the house of Israel.

God's presence was actually manifested as a fire, as it was to Moses at the Burning Bush and to the Israelites on Mt. Sinai.[9] The fire of God's presence was in a cloud to protect the people, because God's presence is fatal to sinful people.[10] By daylight, the people saw only the cloud. At night, they saw God's fire shining through the cloud.

When Moses had the tabernacle constructed and dedicated, the presence of God filled the Holy of Holies in the Tabernacle:

> Then the cloud covered the tent of meeting, and the glory of the Lord filled the tabernacle. Moses was not able to enter the tent of meeting because the cloud had settled on it, and the glory of the Lord filled the tabernacle.[11]

The presence of God dwelt above the Ark of the Covenant in the Holy of Holies and no one was allowed inside.[12] No one could come into God's presence or they would die because God's presence destroys sin and we are riddled with it.

When Solomon dedicated the temple, a similar thing happened:

> It happened that when the priests came from the holy place, the cloud filled the house of the Lord, so that the priests could not stand to minister because of the cloud, for the glory of the Lord filled the house of the Lord.[13]

The presence of the Lord kept even the priests out of the temple, and even Moses out of the tabernacle. No human is holy enough to stand in God's presence.

The separation of God and God's presence from human sin is a basic doctrine of the Bible. It is the reason why the cross of Jesus is necessary. One day we will live directly in God's presence, with no veils or clouds. For that to happen, we need to be cleansed of our sin and made perfect like God is perfect. The cross is God's instrument to accomplish this purpose, which has begun in us who believe, and will be completed at the resurrection of the dead to life at the end of the age.

Yet in the days of Israel, the sinfulness of people was an issue that kept the people separated from God in a visible way at the tabernacle. God was inside and the people outside. A barrier separated the people physically from God's holy presence.

Pollution, Impurity, and Defilement

Leviticus 15:31 and Numbers 5:3 summarize quite well the Bible's doctrine of defilement:

> Thus you shall keep the sons of Israel separated from their uncleanness, so that they will not die in their uncleanness by their defiling My tabernacle that is among them.

> You shall send away both male and female; you shall

send them outside the camp so that they will not defile their camp where I dwell in their midst.

Other scriptures also speak of this idea that the sin of the people pollutes and defiles the sanctuary of God.[14]

Two things in particular caused pollution in God's sanctuary which required cleansing: sin and impurity. We are all familiar with the concept of sin, disobeying God's commandments. It is the concept of impurity that is harder for many to understand. Impurity is not the same as sin, because many of the things considered impure in God's law are not sinful.

God's purity laws are symbolic. At first glance, it is difficult to see rhyme or reason to them. It seems they all had to do with death or loss of life. By making certain things impure, God was showing that he is the God of life, not death:

Causes of Impurity and Their Rationale[15]

Lev. 11: Eating any meat other than the allowed animals.	Restricted death to a handful of species in Israel, so that the land would not be a land of death.
Lev. 12: Childbirth.	Loss of blood is a loss of life.
Lev. 13: Skin Disease.	Causes a person to look like a corpse (whitened skin).
Lev. 14: 33ff. Mildew.	Mildew grows on dead things.
Lev. 15: Semen, Men-struation, and other genital discharges.	Loss of semen or blood is loss of life.
Num. 19: Touching a corpse.	A corpse is death itself and touching a corpse makes one unclean for seven days.

Symbolic impurities, that represented death, polluted God's sanctuary along with sins of the people. God's does not desire for his presence to dwell in the midst of sin and death.

Death was God's punishment for our sin in the Garden. God originally created us for life. Sin is what causes death, and is repugnant to God.

When a woman in the northernmost part of Israel gave birth to a child, her loss of blood symbolically caused pollution at the sanctuary. When a man in the southern regions of Israel cheated his neighbor on a sale, the sanctuary was polluted. It required a cleansing. If the sanctuary was not cleansed often, then God's presence would have to withdraw from the sanctuary and from Israel. That is exactly what happened in the end, in 586 B.C.E., when the sin of Israel hit the breaking point and God abandoned the temple.[16] After that, the Babylonians destroyed the temple and sent the people into exile.

The Cleansing Role of the Sacrifices
Leviticus 1:4 says:

> He shall lay his hand on the head of the burnt offering, that it may be accepted for him to make atonement on his behalf.

Atonement is a word coined in the era of Bible translation standing for "at one" ment, a person being made at one with God.

The Hebrew is *kipper*, a word which has several meanings depending on its form. In one form, the *Qal* form in Hebrew, *kafar* means to cover. Noah, for example, covered (*kafar*) his ark with pitch. Yet in the form that is used of the sacrifices, the *Piel* form in Hebrew, the word means to cleanse or to wipe away.

The fact that *kafar* means to cover has in the past led many commentators to say that the Old Testament sacrifices only covered sin temporarily. Some would say that God did not see the sin because it was covered by the blood.

Yet in sacrificial texts, such as Leviticus 1:4, the word is always used in its other form, a much more common form for this verb, which means to cleanse or wipe away. Sometimes the meaning of a word can best be seen in biblical poetry, where a word is used in parallel with a synonym, such as in Jeremiah 18:23:

> Do not forgive their iniquity or blot out their sin from Your sight.

The word translated "forgive" here is actually *kipper* or atone. It is used in parallel with "blot out."

The sacrifices of Israel did not cover Israel's sin pollution on God's altar. It cleansed it. It blotted it out or wiped it away. The people's sins and impurities polluted the sanctuary and the sacrificial blood cleansed it. (For a more detailed explanation and evidence for this view, see Appendix A: More About the Sacrifices).

The sacrifices of Israel did not bring forgiveness to the worshipper, but cleansed the sanctuary of the worshipper's sins and impurities. The sacrifices of Israel did not make a person clean in God's sight, but they did allow God to live in the midst of the people.

This distinction is crucial to New Testament theology as well as Old Testament. It is why Hebrews 10:4 says, "It is impossible for the blood of bulls and goats to take away sins." Likewise, Hebrews 9:9 says that the sacrifices offered could not cleanse the conscience of the worshipper.

The cross of Jesus was not simply a bigger and better sacrifice modeled on the sacrifices of Leviticus. The cross of Jesus is better by far. The old sacrifices enabled God's presence to be near the people. Jesus' sacrifice enables us to be directly in God's presence. The old sacrifices showed the need for the new, since we needed more than they offered.

This is why Paul was not being inconsistent to believe in Jesus' death for his sin and yet gave sin offerings in Acts 21:26. This is why in the coming temple of Messiah in the days of Jesus' kingdom, the people of the world not yet resurrected will offer sacrifices—so his holy presence can be in their midst.

The Types of Sacrifices and Their Purpose[17]

Lev. 1: The Burnt Offering.	Entire animal burned on altar. Priests keep the skin.	General offering to entreat God for favor or to obtain cleansing.
Lev. 2: The Grain Offering.	Accompanied burnt and peace offerings. Sometimes all burned, usually priests ate part.	For thanksgiving for God's provision. A poor man's purification offering (Lev. 5:11) and possibly a poor man's burnt offering.
Lev. 3: The Peace or Fellowship Offering.	Most of meat eaten by worshipper, parts burnt for God.	An offering for thanksgiving or to complete a vow.
Lev. 4:1-5:13: The Sin or Purification Offering.	Priests ate part of meat. The rest was burnt for God.	To cleanse the sanctuary from the people's sin and impurity.
Lev. 5:14-6:7: The Guilt or Reparation Offering.	Priests ate part of meat. The rest was burnt for God.	To accompany restitution for for stolen goods or goods not tithed on.

Conclusion: Awesome, Inspiring Worship of the Mighty God
The ways of Israel, given by God through Moses and the prophets, were not in any way inferior to our modern ways. In fact, we may all look forward to temple worship in the future.

Cushioned pews or padded, theater style seats are comfortable. Hymnbooks and projector screens with song lyrics are helpful. Colored windows may add a sense of sanctity and worship to a room. Piano music does seem holy, if that is your cultural expectation.

But no one will say that God's temple, rebuilt in Jerusalem in the days of Messiah, will be boring or primitive. Isaiah describes that day:

> Now it will come about that In the last days the mountain of the house of the Lord will be established as the chief of the mountains, and will be raised above the hills; and all the nations will stream to it. And many peoples will come and say, "Come, let us go up to the mountain of the Lord, to the house of the God of Jacob; that He may teach us concerning His ways and that we may walk in His paths." For the law will go forth from Zion and the word of the Lord from Jerusalem.[18]

The house of the Lord is the temple. Isaiah 11 goes on to describe those days further, saying that a shoot will spring from the stem of Jesse, the father of David. He will be the king in those days. The stem from the line of Jesse is none other than Jesus, the Messiah and Son of David. That will be the greatest worship service of all time.

Chapter Five

God's House

A young woman prays in a small group Bible study, "Thank you, God, for your Spirit living inside us. Thank you for letting us draw near, for the tearing of the veil, and the access by which we can boldly come before your throne."

Does this sound rather routine and bland? Or does it stir your passion and sense of thrill?

When Jesus gave up his spirit, Matthew records that "Behold, the veil of the temple was torn in two from top to bottom; and the earth shook and the rocks were split."[1] What happened and is it something we should be excited about?

From Tent-Tabernacle to Palace-Temple

The Israelites worshipped God in a moving structure called the Tabernacle for centuries before there was ever a temple. Similar to the three-part sanctuaries of many Gentile nations, the tabernacle had a courtyard where the people and the priests could gather to perform various tasks of worship.[2] The courtyard was about 150 feet long and seventy-five feet wide.[3]

Towards the back of the courtyard was a tent, which was itself divided inside into two sections. The outer section was the Holy Place, and only priests could enter. At the back of the Holy Place was a veil, and no one could enter into there. It was the Holy of Holies containing the Ark of the Covenant. God's presence dwelt in there and was fatal to any who entered.

By modern standards the tabernacle was not particularly large. In contrast to some temples of the time, it was fairly ordinary. It was moveable because the people were on the move. The command to build the tabernacle came while Israel was in the wilderness. They were to bring it, and God's presence on the Ark of the Covenant, into the Promised Land with them.

When the Israelites did live in the land, the tabernacle moved to various towns, but mostly resided in Shiloh.[4] The faithful in Israel worshipped God wherever the tabernacle was. That was the place on which God chose for his name to dwell.[5]

David, who loved to worship God on a grand scale, had a desire to build a temple for God based on the tabernacle.[6] David saw Jerusalem as the proper city for God to be worshipped in. It was central to the territories of the twelve tribes. It was on a mountain, so it was worshipful to ascend to worship God there. It was a beautiful place, worthy of a temple for God. It was also at or near the place where Abraham had been willing to sacrifice Isaac, Mt. Moriah,[7] and the city where Melchizedek had been king in Abraham's day.[8]

So, David bought a threshing floor there, a place flattened and cleared for the processing of grain, the place where Solomon would build the temple.[9]

Solomon's temple, largely prepared and planned by David, his father, was much grander than the tabernacle. It was larger, taller, and had a lot more gold and bronze to gleam in the Jerusalem sun. After the temple was built, there was no longer a need for the tabernacle, which had been replaced.

The temple, like the tabernacle, was based on the three-part sanctuary model. The courtyard was still the place for daily sacrifices. The outer room of the temple was still a place in which priests performed worship duties daily. And there was still a veil, behind which was the Holy of Holies with the Ark of the Covenant inside.

God's Presence in the Sanctuary

God's presence is more complicated than at first glance. Consider what John says in his gospel, "No one has seen God at any time."[10] Yet we read stories about Moses seeing God and even the Israelites.

Consider Leviticus 9:23, "The glory of the Lord appeared to

all the people." This appearance of God to the people led to a mistake on the part of Nadab and Abihu that was fatal to them.

Consider the story in Exodus 34:29-35, when Moses would come down from the mountain where he had met with God. His face had an afterglow from God's glory that was too bright for the people. Just the afterglow of God's glory from Moses' face threatened to blind them. So the Israelites asked Moses to wear a veil.

It would seem, then, from these two examples, that Moses saw a much more potent form of God than the people. God appeared to the people on a few occasions. In fact, his presence above the tabernacle could be seen day and night in the wilderness.[11] Yet the mere afterglow on Moses' face was too much for the people.

In Numbers 12:7-8, God rebukes Moses' brother and sister for coveting his role as a leader. God says that though he speaks to prophets by visions and dreams:

Not so, with my servant Moses, he is faithful in all my household; with him I speak mouth to mouth, even openly and not in dark sayings, and he beholds the form of the Lord.

Moses beholds God's form in ways that no other prophet does. Clearly there are levels to God's glory, to his presence or his form.

Finally, consider the story of Moses requesting to see God's glory. Moses sees more of God than anyone else and yet he wants more. God says to him in Exodus 33:20-23:

But he said, "You cannot see my face, for no man can see me and live!" Then the Lord said, "Behold, there is a place by me, and you shall stand there on the rock; and it will come about, while my glory is passing by, that I will put you in the cleft of the rock and cover you with my hand until I have passed by. Then I will take my hand away and you shall see my back, but my face shall not be seen."

Could there be any doubt that God's presence has many levels of intensity? God allows some to see him at one level and others at another level. What one person can see might kill another person who is not as privileged.

So it was with God's presence inside the Holy of Holies in the tabernacle and, later, the temple. When God filled the tabernacle with his presence, Moses had to leave the tent because God's glory inside was too much even for him.[12] Similarly, when Solomon dedicated the temple, the levitical choirs and priests had to leave the temple because God's glory was so powerful.[13]

God said of his glory in the Holy of Holies that it was fatal. When instructing the high priest about his duties for Yom Kippur (the Day of Atonement) in Leviticus 16:2, God said, "Tell your brother Aaron that he shall not enter at any time into the holy place inside the veil, before the mercy seat which is on the ark, or he will die; for I will appear in the cloud over the mercy seat."

When the Israelites worshipped at the tabernacle and the temple, this was what made it so special. Beyond the doorway into the sanctuary, on the other side of veil, at the very back of the sanctuary, was God's presence. Just to be that close to it was beyond description for those who loved God.

Names of the Tabernacle

The Bible uses a variety of names for the tabernacle, which all give us insight into its purpose:

Sanctuary	Exodus 25:8	Emphasizing that this was holy space.
Tabernacle	Exodus 25:9	From a Hebrew word meaning to dwell, emphasizing God's dwelling.
Tent	Exodus 26:36	Emphasizing the temporary nature of the dwelling.

Tabernacle of the Congregation	Exodus 29:42	Emphasizing that this is where the people met with God.
Tabernacle of the Testimony	Exodus 38:21	The testimony is a name for the tablets of the commandments stored in the Ark inside the Holy of Holies, emphasizing the Torah.

Layout and Furniture of the Tabernacle

Picture a large courtyard, seventy-five feet wide and twice as long. At the back end, furthest from the gates, is the tent itself. In front of the tent, closest to the gates, is the altar on which the sacrifices are offered. Between the altar and the tent is a basin for the priests to wash hands and feet before entering the tent.

As an ordinary Israelite, you would not be allowed inside the tent. If you could go inside, you would see three pieces of furniture in a room with a veil at the back. To your left would be the Menorah, a seven-branched lampstand with olive oil lamps. To your right you would see a table with twelve giant loaves of bread called the Bread of the Presence. At the back would be a small golden altar with a censer on top. On this altar there would be fragrant smoke of incense, a special formula forbidden for any other use. Behind the veil, you know there would be the Ark of the Covenant. Its top was made of gold and featured two cherubim facing one another with wingtips spread toward each other.

The furniture of the tabernacle is full of purpose and meaning:

Altar of Burnt Offering, Exod. 27:1-8	The place where God's fire was maintained (Lev. 6:12, 9:24), sacrificial blood dashed, and sacrificial portions burned. The altar represents the need for cleansing in order for God's presence to be near.

Laver/Basin, Exod. 30:17-21	The system for the priests to wash hands and feet before entering the tent. The concept may be that the sins of the people clung to the hands and feet of the priests or merely that the priest's own sins and impurities needed cleansing before entering the tent. The washing of hands and feet in addition to the blood cleansing of the twice-daily offering suggests that specific cleansing is needed when men draw even nearer to God.
Bread of the Presence/ Showbread, Exod. 25:23-30	Twelve loaves represent the twelve tribes. Oil and wine were also placed on the table. This combined with the name suggests that these were kept in God's presence and refreshed weekly as a memorial from the twelve tribes, remembering God's provision of grain, oil, and produce. Unlike other nations, Israel made no pretense that their God ate the bread or needed food, but the table served as Israel's perpetual thanksgiving to God.
Menorah / Lampstand, Exod. 25:31-40	Seven branches suggest seven days of creation and God's power. Light is always present in God's glory in Torah. Whereas God's glory dwelt in the Holy of Holies, the light of the Menorah was a symbol of that glory in the outer room of the tent.
Altar of Incense, Exod. 30:1-10	God's glory in Torah is always covered with a cloud to protect humankind from God's fatal holiness. Leviticus 16:13 says that the incense cloud had to precede the High Priest going into the Holy of Holies or he would die. Normally the incense was in the outer room in

	front of the veil going into the Holy of Holies. The incense represents man's needed protection from the glory of God.
Ark of the Covenant, Exod. 25:10-22	This square box with golden statues of cherubim represents God's throne and footstool. Cherubim are heavenly beings with flaming swords who guard the presence of God, as they guarded the Garden in Eden after the fall. They are present for two reasons: (1) they guard the presence of God dwelling above the Ark and (2) their outstretched wings form a throne for God's presence. The Ark is said to be God's footstool (1 Chron. 28:2). In the Ark are the tablets of the ten commandments, representing God's covenant with Israel. In the Ancient Near East, kings sometimes kept treaties and oaths in the footstools of pagan gods.[14] The meaning was to ensure God's loyalty to the covenant promises to Israel.

Allegories and Types Suggested for the Tabernacle's Meaning
How are we to interpret the tabernacle furniture? Are there hidden meanings? Is the tabernacle an elaborate allegory or type of the cross of Jesus?

There is a common approach to teaching about the tabernacle which looks for symbolic meaning in every detail. The tabernacle is thought of as a clue or a hint to the sacrificial death of Jesus for sin.

A very simple version could see the articles of the tabernacle as follows:

- Altar = Christ's redemptive work on the cross.
- Laver/Basin = Christ's work of sanctification, washing of water by the word (Eph. 5:26).

- Bread of the Presence/Showbread = Christ, the bread of heaven.
- Menorah/Lampstand = Christ, light of the world.
- Incense = Christ's prayers on our behalf.

It is possible to get very specific about the detailed symbolism. For example, one writer says that the altar is made of Shittim (Acacia) wood because it is a "hard, incorruptible, indestructible wood" corresponding to "the humanity of Christ, who came from a root out of dry ground . . . and was sinless . . . withstood the fire of crucifixion . . . and the decaying effect of the grave." The flesh hooks used by the priests to move animal carcasses "represented the cruel hands of the men who nailed Christ to the cross."[15]

I would suggest this approach is not helpful nor is it accurate. As soon as you start making symbols out of things the Bible describes literally, you can incur error. A symbol can be taken to mean almost anything. Furthermore, this way of reading the tabernacle is backwards. It starts with the New Testament truth and goes back searching for evidence and symbols. It is better to take God's revelation in the order he gave it. Start with the Old Testament and see how it moves forward into the new.

That means we should interpret the tabernacle as it would have been understood in its own time and culture. We should see what the Old Testament says about the tabernacle. Then we will see how it may point to the New Testament without reading back into it.

A Literal Interpretation of the Tabernacle's Meaning
The most important issues in the Tabernacle, understood within Old Testament and its culture, are:

1. The dwelling of God.
2. Holiness, purity, and sacrifice.
3. Drawing near to God.

All of these themes come from the text itself, not human imagination, and relate to the culture of Israel and the Ancient Near East.

The clear message of the tabernacle is that God cannot simply be approached on human terms. God's holiness is fatal to sinful men. His presence dwells within an inner chamber of the tabernacle, approachable only once a year by the High Priest with blood and incense. The closer you move to the inner chamber where God's presence dwells, the fewer people who can enter:

- In front of the courtyard … Anyone can come near.
- Inside the courtyard … Only those bringing offerings or doing the priestly work may enter.
- Inside the tent … Only the priests doing the work of the tabernacle may enter.
- Inside the Holy of Holies … No one may enter.

This message of the tabernacle does relate to Messiah. Messiah's death and resurrection are the means which make it possible for man to dwell with God. The idea that man is not capable of being in God's direct presence without purification flows from the Torah into New Testament teaching.

The concepts of purity abound in the tabernacle. Priests must wash before entering the tent. Sacrificial blood must be dashed against the altar and sometimes in the tent and once a year in the Holy of Holies. The purity laws of Israel have to do with God's holiness. He is separate from sin and death (all purity laws relate to death or the loss of life). He is the God of righteousness and life.

So Messiah can be understood in this way. His death is a purification, not of the altar or the sanctuary as in the Old Testament, but of the believer. Every person is in need of a personal purification.

God's dwelling with his people is central to the tabernacle. The whole land of Israel, with the tabernacle as the spiritual center, is holy. God dwells in the tabernacle so that the people may sense their nearness to him. Yet the sins and impurities of the people pollute the tabernacle and must be continually cleansed with sacrifices. All that can be accomplished through this system is the people being able to draw near to God hidden in a tent.

This relates to Messiah's work as well, for the idea must occur that if we are to live with God in the Age to Come, something better than the tabernacle must come. Instead of God dwelling in a tent, hidden from direct contact, there must be some way for us to directly live with him. This is where Messiah's redemption is seen to be superior and the next step from the work of the tabernacle.

Finally, the tabernacle is about humankind drawing near to God. God made us in his image and to have relationship with him. The tabernacle is the place to which the Israelites came for three annual festivals (Passover, Shavuot (Weeks), and Sukkot (Tabernacles)) to worship before God and enjoy his provision in a great feast.

This too is fulfilled in Messiah, who brings us near to God. Through him, we will worship God in the Age to Come directly and without separation.

The dwelling of God	Messiah brought us the Holy Spirit who now lives in us (John 14:17; 16:7) and we are God's temple (1 Cor. 3:16). This does not, however, negate the fact that God will again dwell in a Temple in Jerusalem (Isaiah 2:2-3; Ezekiel 40-48).
Holiness, purity	Messiah cleansed us from our sins and sent the Spirit to sanctify us (1 John 1:9; Rom. 6:22).
Sacrifice, altar	Messiah's death was a better kind of sacrifice, cleansing us, not just the sanctuary, so that we can live directly in God's presence (Heb. 9:9-10, 14; 10:4).
Laver/Basin	Messiah cleanses us from sin and makes us pure in God's presence.

Bread of the Presence	This continues to represent for us the joyful thanksgiving we should give to God.
Menorah	The Menorah was a symbol in the outer room of God's glory in the Holy of Holies. So when Messiah came we "beheld the glory" (John 1:14) for he is the "radiance of the glory of God and his exact imprint" (Heb. 1:3).
Incense	The incense protected the priests from God's fatal holiness. So Jesus is our advocate and protection so that we may draw near to God (1 John 2:1-2).
Holy of Holies	The way into God has been opened by Jesus (Mark 15:38) so that we may boldly come right before God's throne (Heb. 4:16).
Ark	Jesus brought the New Covenant of God (Luke 22:20) with better promises that that of Moses (Heb. 8:6). Jesus is God's presence manifest to us and he sent the Spirit of God to dwell in us, so that the Ark of the Covenant is no longer needed (Jer. 3:16).

The Tabernacle and the Cross
Temples Past: Solomon, Zerubbabel, and Herod

Israel worshipped God at the tabernacle from the days of Moses until the days of Solomon. Solomon built the temple to replace the tabernacle, but based on the same model. The duties of the Levites changed from being movers of the tabernacle to being the musicians, singers, and servants of the temple. 1 Kings 7-8 and 2 Chronicles 2-7 describe in detail Solomon's building and dedicating the temple.

Among other things that Solomon said during this period is that God's people in foreign lands should pray towards Jerusalem and the temple. Solomon asked that God would answer prayers especially by Jews directed toward the temple.[16] It continues to be a Jewish custom, and a good one for non-Jews also, to pray toward Jerusalem. Daniel did this in Babylon.[17] From the United States and Europe, the direction for such prayer is east.

Solomon's temple was completely destroyed in 586 B.C.E., as detailed by the end of the books of Kings and foretold in prophets such as Jeremiah. The end foretold for disobedient Israel even as early as Deuteronomy 30 had come upon them.

Under the leadership of Zerubbabel, the temple was rebuilt seventy years after it had been destroyed.[18] Yet this temple was less glorious than Solomon's. So, starting shortly before the birth of Jesus, Herod the Great began expanding and improving the temple. Even though Herod rebuilt the temple, it was still considered the second temple and not the third. The third temple is coming any day, in preparation for the return of Messiah.

The Coming Temple of Messiah

In numerous places the Bible foretells a future temple. Paul speaks of a future temple in 2 Thessalonians 2:4, where anti-Christ will exalt himself.

The most beautiful promises and descriptions of the future temple are in the prophets. Isaiah and Micah both speak of the last days when the Gentile nations will come up the to mountain of the house of the Lord.[19] The house of the Lord is a term for the temple. From this house, Messiah will judge the Gentile nations with fairness and justice.

The most detailed description of Messiah's temple comes in Ezekiel 40-48. Many interpreters, convinced that the temple is the past and sacrifices have no place in Messiah's kingdom, try to find another explanation for these chapters. Yet, taken literally, they describe in great detail the measurements and new worship regulations for a temple that has never been built. God does not make mistakes. The temple Ezekiel describes has to be the temple of Messiah.

And Ezekiel says some wonderful things about that temple. A river will flow from it and make the Dead Sea alive and produce trees that will heal the nations.[20] From the temple of Messiah Jesus there will flow life and healing, just as in the days when he walked among us before. He is our life and our healer.

God's Presence in the Old and New Covenant

Unfortunately, if people do not study the literal truth of the tabernacle and temple, it is difficult or impossible to understand the blessings of the New Covenant.

Israelites rejoiced at the chance to stand anywhere near to the temple, to even be close enough to hear the priests at a distance or see the smoke of the offerings. That was almost as close to God as they would get.

To bring an offering meant to stand even closer. You were between the altar and the sanctuary. You were in easy sight of the door into the sanctuary itself. God's presence was behind a door and a veil. To be that close would raise the hairs on your neck.

Yet no one could get closer. Until at Jesus' death, the Father tore the veil in two. Rabbinic tradition does not mention the veil being torn, but does mention some changes at the temple starting in the year Jesus died. The doors of the temple would no longer stay closed. The red yarn which God miraculously turned white each Yom Kippur ceased to do so.[21]

Something had fundamentally changed. The writer of Hebrews did not miss it. In Hebrews 10:20 he referred to "a new and living way which He inaugurated for us through the veil, that is, His flesh."

Now we have God inside of us. We are temples ourselves. And no door or veil separates us from his direct presence. What a faithful Israelite longed for, like Moses asking to see God's glory, we have by faith.

So we can pray, like the woman at the beginning of this

chapter, "Thank you, God, for your Spirit living inside us. Thank you for letting us draw near, for the tearing of the veil and the access by which we can boldly come before your throne."

Interlude

Jesus Versus Satan

To a young man raised in Galilee the Judean desert was especially harsh. The hills and limestone mountains of Galilee were covered with trees and shrubs and grass. Many times Jesus had made the short journey to the Sea of Galilee. Water and life were abundant.

But the Judean desert was baked hard so that a man's shins ached from walking on the stony ground. The hills were so extreme and unforgiving constant caution was needed when walking through this barren region.

Tendrils like snakes writhed from the ground, coils of heat reflecting off of the hard clay. Thirst came quickly and perspiration soaked his clothes.

The Spirit ordered him here right after the immersion in the Jordan. From cool waters and the voice of heaven, Jesus came to this painful place.

He was weak, faint from a fast forty days long. He took comfort in knowing the end of the fast was near.

Then the evil one came. Jesus was familiar with many forms of Satan. Now, with Jesus in bodily form, he saw Satan in a new way. He experienced the evil one as a man experiences him. Raw power and evil gave his body an unfamiliar sensation, a heightened awareness that in most men would be the start of fear.

"If you are the Son of God, tell this stone to become bread," Satan's voice came with a concealed sneer. For the first time in history, the Son of God was under Satan's spell. The Father gave Satan great authority in this moment. Jesus could see visions of bread projected by the evil one.

It wasn't merely the presence of the evil one that alerted Jesus to the falseness of the proposal. Evil and wrong were always clear to Jesus. To end the test by using unlimited power in such a trivial way was wrong. The fast was not over.

The words came naturally to Jesus' lips. He had written them by the hand of Moses before his earthly sojourn. Yet once on earth, Jesus learned the scriptures in the same way as other men. As a boy in Nazareth, the words of God were recited and memorized.

The words that came to him now were familiar from recent participation in the synagogue. The words of Moses were read every week. The readings shortly before the time of Jesus' fast in the desert had been from Deuteronomy. "It is written, 'Man must not live on bread alone.'" The evil one retreated.

Jesus had peace for a few more hours until the prince of darkness came again. Yet when he looked at him, Jesus could not now see the darkness. Instead, he appeared as an angel of light. The Father was letting Satan show his glory even to the Son of God.

Jesus was lifted in Spirit by Satan's power. The Father had lifted Ezekiel and other prophets in the Spirit. Satan now mimicked the Father's power. The prince of light pointed with a powerful hand to the centers of the world's kingdoms. Rome lay before him and the Parthians and many other kingdoms.

"I will give you their splendor and all this authority," the brilliant prince promised, "because it has been given over to me, and I can give it to anyone I want. If you, then, will worship me, all will be yours."

He was right. The Father had given Satan dominion over the world. Yet it was only for a time. Jesus could see Satan's design. The Son of God would be a strong ally against the Father.

Again the words from the Torah scroll in the synagogue came to him. They were from the same part of Deuteronomy. "It is written, 'Worship the Lord, your God, and serve him only.'" Again the devil retreated.

This time the peace was short-lived. Jesus' last day of fasting would not leave him any rest. The shining prince was now darker and more terrible. His evil somehow seemed majestic in the form he now chose.

Taking Jesus by the hand, he flew him bodily to Jerusalem. As they neared, somehow the other people took no notice of Satan or Jesus. He was woozy from the weakness of the fast. When the devil placed him on the corner of the temple looking down to a fall that would cause certain death, Jesus felt his body sway. His body was prone to death like any man's.

The devil saw the physical weakness and obviously was pleasured by it. "If you are the Son of God," he said, "throw yourself down from here. For it is written . . ."

The words penetrated Jesus soul like a Roman spear. They were the words of the Psalms. They were the words of the Spirit. The devil was fighting scripture with scripture, beauty with beauty, and truth with true words distorted in application.

The Psalm was beautiful. "He will give his angels orders concerning you to protect you." The fair ones of God, the messengers of the Most High, they would serve Jesus in his moment of need. "They will support you with their hands . . ."—yes, it was true. They would not let the Son of God fall—". . . so that you will not strike your foot against a stone."

Jesus saw the distortion, obvious and ugly next to God's beautiful promise. The final time for quoting Deuteronomy was at hand. "It is said, 'Do not test the Lord your God.'"

A supernatural cry of rage faded into oblivion as Satan was swept away this time. The Father removed him and no power of the devil could resist the power of the One.

Jesus felt himself falling, but he was no longer on the corner of the temple. He was in the Judean desert again. And he did not hit the ground. The angels the devil had spoken of in the Psalm, they caught the Son of God. They fed him. The fast was over.

Chapter Six

Commandments, Law, Grace

The rabbis count 613 commandments in the Torah, the five books of Moses. If you try to count you may arrive at a different number. Decisions have to be made about what counts as a separate commandment.

The number 613 has symbolic significance. There are 365 positive commandments and 248 prohibitions. The 365 positive commandments correspond to the number of days in a year and the 248 prohibitions correspond to the number of bones and organs in the body.

To some people, 613 commandments might seem like a lot. In fact, many of the 613 are commands concerning festivals and temple procedures. Many of them cannot be kept literally today. Besides, according to the Dakes Bible, there are more than 1,000 commandments in the New Testament.[1]

Common Misgivings About the Law

The law of Moses gets a bad rap. Few people are aware or give much credence to the positive statements of Jesus and Paul about the Torah:

> *Do not think that I came to abolish the Law or the Prophets; I did not come to abolish but to fulfill. For truly I say to you, until heaven and earth pass away, not the smallest letter or stroke shall pass from the Law until all is accomplished.*[2]

The scribes and the Pharisees have seated themselves in the chair of Moses; therefore all that they tell you, do and observe, but do not do according to their deeds; for they say things and do not do them.[3]

Woe to you, scribes and Pharisees, hypocrites! For you tithe mint and dill and cummin, and have neglected the weightier provisions of the law: justice and mercy and faithfulness; but these are the things you should have done without neglecting the others.[4]

For we know that the Law is spiritual, but I am of flesh, sold into bondage to sin.[5]

Jesus and Paul viewed the law of Moses as spiritual and having continuing validity.

To take a complex issue and simplify it, there are two very common views of the law of Moses: the Reformed view and the Dispensationalist view. In the Reformed view, the laws of Moses need to be subdivided into categories of moral, civil, and ceremonial law. Only the moral law is still in force as God's law today. In the Dispensationalist view, the entire law of Moses has been fulfilled or is obsolete. None of it is in force. Only the New Testament commandments are in force as God's law today.

Many people take a little from each view. Especially difficult for most people to deal with are the Ten Commandments. Most people feel they are important, but one of them is not a moral issue at all: the Sabbath. Thus, some try to change the Biblical teaching about the Sabbath to either change it to Sunday or make it mean any day of rest at all.

There is another way of looking at the law of Moses that is more complex but which answers the relevant issues more completely. We could call it the Messianic Jewish view of the law. To be sure, within Messianic Jewish groups there are also disagreements about this issue, but a consensus may be emerging.

The law of Moses is God's covenant with Israel and is still in effect. The law of Moses has nothing to do with salvation, but with Israel's blessing. Many of the commandments in the law of Moses have universal application to Jews and Gentiles, but some are strictly for Jews. Thus, for example, Gentiles need not be circumcised, as the New Testament makes clear. Many of the laws cannot be applied in the modern situation because the situation has changed. Thus, for example, sacrifices cannot be offered without a temple and a functioning priesthood.

This means that a student of the Bible studying the laws should always be aware of certain questions:

1. Is this commandment limited to Israel? Does God indicate that it is a sign between himself and Israel (Sabbath in Exodus 31:13, Circumcision in Genesis 17:11, etc.)? Does God assume or allow Gentiles to break it (dietary law in Deuteronomy 14:21)?
2. Is this commandment inoperable because it cannot be applied? Has something changed that makes it impossible to keep (no priests or judges in the land of Israel, no temple, not in the wilderness anymore, etc.)? Does it reflect a situation that is no longer in effect (slavery in Exodus 21)?

The reader is encouraged to read my other book, *Paul Didn't Eat Pork*, for a detailed examination of New Testament teaching about the law of Moses.

Meanwhile, there are some myths and truths about the law that every Bible student should consider:

Myths	Truths
The Old Testament laws are designed to be impossible in order to drive people to the cross.	God does not give burdensome commands (1 John 5:3). The hardest commandment is to love the Lord with all our heart.

Myths	Truths
The Old Testament laws are too difficult to understand. The Old Testament laws are designed to keep Jews and Gentiles apart. This goes against the New Testament teaching of unity.	They require patience, good reference tools, and an understanding of how the law works. It was Jewish tradition, not Biblical law, that kept Gentiles out of the temple. God always allowed it (Num. 15:14).
The Old Testament laws are devoid of grace.	They are full of grace. God forgave sin numerous times. He ordained the sacrifices within the law to help Israel stay in his love.
The Old Testament laws were a system for Israel to earn salvation by doing good deeds.	The books of Moses do not speak directly of salvation or afterlife. The law was Israel's code for living and as a nation they could be blessed by keeping God's ways. The law never had anything to do with salvation.
The laws about the festivals and the temple are obsolete.	They will come back with some changes in the Messianic Age.
It is wrong for a Jewish believer in Jesus to insist on keeping the Sabbath or the dietary laws.	It is wrong for a Jewish believer in Jesus to abandon God's commandments for his people.
Advocates of the law of Moses are trying to get churches to start acting like Jews and worshipping on Saturdays.	Perhaps some are, but mature Messianic Jewish theology recognizes that Gentiles should not be told to live like Jews.

What's in the Law?

The law is a broad term that could be used to refer to the whole Torah (the five books of Moses) or simply to the commandment portions of the Torah.

If we mean by law the whole Torah, then it contains much more than commandments. The story of creation, the fall, the covenant with Abraham and the patriarchs, and the stories of Israel's redemption, journeys, and failures take up most of the space in the law. Further, a great deal of space is consumed with detailed descriptions of the tabernacle and the priestly procedures for sacrifices.

If we consider simply the commandments, even then we find that they occur throughout the Torah and not just in legal passages. For example, the commandment for Israelites to circumcise their sons occurs in Genesis 17 as part of the Abraham story. The commandment about Nazirite vows occurs in Numbers 6, as part of the details about the holiness and order of the wilderness encampment of Israel.

In many ways, the law is summarized by the Ten Commandments. In fact, some scholars have suggested that the Ten Commandments are the organizing scheme of Deuteronomy.[6] Deuteronomy is the retelling of the commandments and contains most of them repeated from earlier scriptures:

First Commandment	No other Gods.	Deut 6-11. Laws about the one and only God and how to relate to him.
Second Commandment	No idols.	Deut 12. Laws about getting rid of hilltop shrines and having only one temple. Laws against following practices of Canaanites.
Third Commandment	Using God's name as holy.	Deut 13:1 – 14:21. Laws about false prophets and false teachers who promote

		idolatry. Dietary laws about holiness.
Fourth Commandment	Honor the Sabbath.	Deut 14:22 – 16:17. Laws about tithing, Sabbath years, and festivals.
Fifth Commandment	Honor father and mother.	Deut 16:18 – 18:22. Laws about judges, officers, kings, justice, and temple authorities.
Sixth Commandment	Do not murder.	Deut 19-21. Laws about cities of refuge, land disputes, and warfare.
Seventh Commandment	Do not commit adultery.	Deut 22:1 – 23:14. Laws about mixing things, faithfulness to your neighbor, sexual sins and crimes, and purity regarding sexual and bodily functions.
Eighth Commandment	Do not steal.	Deut 23:15 – 24:7. Laws about helping escaped slaves, prohibiting interest, paying vows, and a woman's rights in divorce.
Ninth Commandment	Do not give false testimony.	Deut 24:8-16. Caution in determining skin disease. Laws against keeping a neighbor's pledge for a loan. Laws against punishing the innocent.
Tenth Commandment	You shall not covet.	Deut 24:17 – 26:15. Laws protecting widows and orphans, leaving gleanings for the poor, just weights, and first fruits.

Love in the Law

The Torah is definitely a book of love. It is in Deuteronomy 6:5 that God commanded us to "love the Lord your God with all your heart and will all your soul and with all your might." It is in Leviticus 19:18 that God said, "Love your neighbor as yourself."

The commandments can all be summarized by these two commands. Thus, in the Ten Commandments, numbers one through four are about loving God. Numbers five through ten are about loving your neighbor. All of the commandments of the law can be seen in these categories. The Torah is about love.

The commandment to love God is amazing. We are commanded to love God with all of our:

1. Heart (*Levav*, in Hebrew)—Refers to our thinking and emotions.
2. Soul (*nefesh*, in Hebrew)—Refers to our total being, not soul in the Greek sense of the word.
3. Might (*me'od*, in Hebrew)—Refers to intensity or "muchness," and means with everything we have.

In other words, we are to love God with all of our being: our thinking, feeling, and choosing (mind, emotions, and will) as well as our bodies. And we are to do so with all the intensity that we possess.

The command is all-consuming. Some might say it is ridiculous. It is impossible to completely keep, though we are expected to. You cannot love God too much.

To love God with our thinking is to get to know him, like we get to know a person we are thinking of marrying. To love him with our emotions is to learn to express our feelings to God, much like learning to show love for a spouse. To love God with our choosing is the hardest part. We need the thinking and feeling love to give us strength to choose God's way over our own.

The command to love our neighbor as ourselves is different. It is not an all-consuming command. People don't deserve the same level of love as God. Yet the Torah makes it clear that loving God is evidenced by loving people. The two go together. When you, in humility, prefer others over yourself or when you help your enemy in his time of need, you are showing God the kind of love he desires.

Far from being a sterile book of laws and rituals, the Torah is a book of love. Jesus called these two commands the greatest of all.

Faith in the Law

It is in the Torah that we see faith or trust in God as the crucial means of being in God's favor. Genesis 15:6 says, "[Abraham] believed in the Lord, and he reckoned it to him as righteousness."

Faith is all through the Torah. When Israel is complaining in the wilderness, God says of them, "How long will they not believe in me, despite all the signs which I have performed in their midst?"[7] Moses says of the people, "You did not trust the Lord your God."[8]

Israel learns in several places that they are chosen by God. They did not earn their place. For example, God says, "Yet on your fathers did the Lord set his affection to love them, and he chose their descendants after them, even you above all peoples."[9]

God emphasizes to the people that obeying his commandments is not too hard for them. He says of the commandment, "It is not in heaven, that you should say, 'Who will go up to heaven for us to get it for us and make us hear it, that we may observe it?' Nor is it beyond the sea, that you should say, 'Who will cross the sea for us to get it for us and make us hear it, that we may observe it?' But the word is very near you, in your mouth and in your heart, that you may observe it."[10] Paul uses this very text in Romans 10:5-10 to prove that salvation comes by believing and confessing. Moses was helping Israel understand that God did not expect impossible obedience, but submitted hearts. God grants righteousness based on faith and repentance, not performance.

Perhaps the greatest picture of faith in the Torah is the Passover. The people had to believe something amazing: that the God of their ancestors would set them free from the most powerful kingdom on earth. They had to believe that a death angel was coming on the night of Passover. They had to show their faith by placing blood on the doorpost. It was their faith, not their performance, that saved them.

Changes in the Law

The laws and commandments of God were always understood to change and adapt to situations. For example, when Israel was in the wilderness, all camped very close to the tabernacle. God gave this law:

> *Any man from the house of Israel who slaughters an ox or a lamb or a goat in the camp, or who slaughters it outside the camp, and has not brought it to the doorway of the tent of meeting to present it as an offering to the Lord before the tabernacle of the Lord, bloodguiltiness is to be reckoned to that man. He has shed blood and that man shall be cut off from among his people.*[11]

In other words, the people were forbidden to slaughter meat for eating except as a peace offering at the tabernacle.

Yet the law changed in Deuteronomy as the people were about to go into the land. Many of them would live several days' journey away from the tabernacle. It would not be practical for them to only eat meat when they could slaughter it at the sanctuary. So, in Deuteronomy 12:15, God granted that the people could eat meat slaughtered in their towns. The situation changed and the Torah changed.

Another example of this phenomenon can be seen in the duties of the Levites. Numbers 4 describes in detail the work of the different families of Levites. Most of their work had to do with the moving of the tabernacle and its furniture.

Yet a change came in the days of King David. David moved the tabernacle to Jerusalem where it was permanently stationed. There would be no more moving it around. So David said:

The Lord God of Israel has given rest to his people, and he dwells in Jerusalem forever. Also, the Levites will no longer need to carry the tabernacle and all its utensils for its service.[12]

So David changed their duties. They became primarily musicians and singers to lead the people in public worship.

Thus, it is no problem at all when a modern interpreter of the law of Moses notes that certain laws can no longer be observed. Changes in situation call for changes in the Torah.

This is what the writer of Hebrews referred to when he said, "When the priesthood is changed, of necessity there takes place a change of law also."[13] The New Testament was not overthrowing the law, but noting that there were changes. Jesus is a high priest of a different order, one not legislated by the Torah. His priesthood represents a change in the law, whereby the High Priest is no longer a descendant of Levi and Aaron. Jesus changed the situation and the law changed. Yet there will still be a levitical priesthood in the days of Messiah.[14]

Troubling Passages in the Law

There are some parts of the law that are troubling for modern readers. These types of passages lead some people to assume that the law of Moses is inferior, unworthy of our devotion and study. Yet this cannot be. God's word is all pure and holy. Nowhere does the Bible teach that part of the Bible is inferior.

The law is spiritual, as Paul said in Romans 7:14. The troubling parts of the law will turn out to be good and pure upon closer examination.

One example of a troubling passage is in Numbers 5:11-31. This passage commands a test when a woman is accused of adultery without witnesses. The priest puts a little dirt from the floor of the tabernacle into water. He pours the water over a written list of curses and into a bowl. The woman then drinks the dirty water.

If she swells in the abdomen and thins in the thighs, becoming barren, then everyone will know she was guilty.

This seems like a sort of witch-trial. It raises questions such as why the man has no test if the woman is suspicious. How could this be in God's word?

The intent of this law is to protect women from false accusations of adultery. There is no test for the men, because in ancient society men held all the power. A woman had no recourse against her husband for cheating unless there were witnesses. But even without witnesses a man could deprive a woman of her rights to marital relations and children.

In fact, upon examination, this was the opposite of a witch trial. The woman was presumed innocent unless proven guilty by a miraculous affliction. There is no telling how many women were spared the wrath of jealous husbands by this piece of Torah.

Another troubling passage is Exodus 21:2-11 about Hebrew slavery. The very idea of slavery is a repugnant violation of human freedom. To enslave someone is to deprive them of their humanity.

Yet on close examination, it turns out Hebrew slaves were temporary debt-slaves. They could sell themselves due to extreme debt or they could be sold if unable to make restitution for a theft.[15] Furthermore, in the passage about female slaves was a way to help girls in poor families. The father could sell his daughter as a slave, but the owner was to take her as his wife or his son's wife upon adulthood. She was then to be treated as a wife with full rights.

Some troubling passages involve God protecting people from abusive customs. We might ask why God did not forbid the customs, such as capturing war brides or husbands putting away their wives. Jesus indicates that God allowed some practices because he knew men would not stop doing them.[16]

So instead of forbidding them, God put protections in place for the good of the oppressed. War brides must be allowed time to mourn the death of their families and cannot be sold as slaves.[17]

Women put away in divorce received a certificate so that they could remarry and the man could not take her back (thus making a man think before hastily sending her away).[18]

Upon study and examination, even the most troubling passages of the Torah are good and spiritual. God's word is good and pure, all of it from Genesis to Revelation.

And the law is the foundation of the entire Bible. By failing to study Genesis through Deuteronomy, any Bible student will be weak in understanding. Creation, covenant, blood sacrifice, worship, justice, and even prophecy are all sourced in the books of Moses. To fail to understand them is to fail to properly understand the rest of the Bible.

Chapter Seven

God the Warrior
and King

It is a little known secret of the historical books of the Old Testament that the main characters are not people like Joshua, Gideon, David, Solomon, Elijah, or Hezekiah.

The books of Joshua, Judges, Ruth, 1 and 2 Samuel, 1 and 2 Kings, 1 and 2 Chronicles, Ezra, Nehemiah, and Esther have a different main character. They are not biographies of the people involved. They are history explained with the divine purpose in mind. In other words, God is the main character.

Do you want to know how God responds when people obey him? How does he take action when people rebel? What sins does he take most seriously? How does his forgiveness look in action? How does he handle imperfect obedience? How does he keep his promises? How does he view authority and responsibility?

What better way to learn these things than to see God in action? The historical books are more like a biography of God than the human characters. To be more accurate, they are prophetic history.

In fact, in the Jewish way of dividing the Bible, they are called the Former Prophets. How can history be prophetic? Remember that prophecy is not just foretelling future events. Prophecy involved any inspired message from God. When the biblical historians wrote, God gave them prophetic insight into the meaning and purpose of events in the history of Israel and Judah.

To better understand the historical books and what they are saying about God and about Israel, we will learn:

1. The historical outline of Israel and Judah.
2. The types of prose in the historical narratives.
3. The basic theology of the historical books.

A Basic Outline of History

The Patriarchs
c. 2100-1900 B.C.E.
Jacob into Egypt ------------- 70 Israelites.

The Exodus
c. 1440 B.C.E. (or c. 1290 B.C.E.).

Conquest/Joshua 1400 B.C.E. ---- Judges until 1043 B.C.E.
Or 1250 B.C.E. until 1043 B.C.E.

United Monarchy
Saul 1043 B.C.E.
David 1011 B.C.E.
Solomon 971 B.C.E.

Divided Monarchy
Jeroboam-Israel (North)	Rehoboam-Judah
931 to 722 B.C.E.	931 to 586 B.C.E.
19 Kings, all bad.	20 kings, some godly.
722 B.C.E. Israel destroyed	586 B.C.E. Judah destroyed by
Assyria. People intermarried.	Babylon. People in exile.

538 B.C.E. Return under Zerubbabel – Persian Period Begins.
516 B.C.E. Temple Rebuilt
(Second Temple).
Malachi c. 475 B.C.E.
Chronicles-Ezra-Nehemiah
Written c. 400 B.C.E.

The historical books begin after Moses' death on Mt. Nebo, unable to enter the Promised Land. Joshua, his protégé, leads the people in the spirit of Moses. The people conquer a few cities necessary to gain a foothold in the land. A careful reading of Joshua and Judges shows that they did not rid the land of Canaanites. Nonetheless, they were living in the land, keeping away from the powerful Canaanite cities. Not until David would the conquest be complete.

In the period of Judges, the Israelites paid the price for not finishing the task God set for them. They entered a cycle of sin, judgment, repentance, and salvation by God using human rulers. Ruth is a story of an unusually godly man, Boaz, in the midst of the wicked period of Judges. Boaz and his Moabite wife, Ruth, produce the line of David.

In Samuel, Israel got their first kings. First they had the king the people would have chosen, Saul, tall and good looking. Saul was destined to be a failure because he was not a king after God's heart. David was the king who had what God desired: passionate worship, absolute faith, hatred for idolatry, and submission to God as the real king.

Kings is the chronicle of Israel splitting into two nations. It is primarily a story of degeneration from David's worshipful kingdom to Israel and Judah's destruction. A few bright spots happened along the way in Judah. In Israel, the only bright spot was the time of Elijah and Elisha, who were not kings but prophets.

Ezra and Nehemiah tell the story of the Judahites who returned from Babylon. The temple was rebuilt exactly seventy years after it was destroyed, just as God had said.

Esther is a story set in the Persian period. Mordechai and Esther are called Jews—the first time that term was used. They had not returned to Judah, but chose to stay in Persia, indicating a probable short-sightedness in their faith. Nonetheless, God works through them anonymously and saves the Jews in Persia.

The historical books span between 850 and 1,000 years, depending on the interpretation of dates. They do not reveal a picture of an obedient Israel, following God's law. Rather, they reveal a people who followed God half-heartedly while sacrificing to idols on high places also. They point to the truth of the sinfulness of humankind. They also point to the faithfulness and grace of God, who keeps his promises and gives favor to undeserving Israel.

In short, the history of Israel agrees completely with the gospel. In these stories we find much to parallel our own experience. Even the people of God do not follow him wholeheartedly. Yet there are blessed exceptions, like David, Elijah, and Josiah. And they inspire us.

The Types of Prose in the Historical Books

The student of the Bible should be aware of the fact that it is a book. Great literature, such as the Bible, uses many tools to communicate meaning. We can get great insight into the message of the historical books by paying attention to the types of prose contained in them:

1. Dialogue.
2. Narration of action.
3. Narration of character.
4. Narration of divine intent.

The historical narratives of the Bible strongly prefer to use dialogue to advance the story. They like to show rather than tell. They assume the reader will see through the lines of the characters' words. They expect us to see dishonesty as well as faith. We often see character and meaning in the way the people interact through dialogue. We're helped in recognizing dialogue by English translations which, fairly accurately, place quotation marks around the dialogue.

In addition to dialogue, there is a narrator's voice adding information to the story. The narrator gives us three kinds of information. First, he narrates action to show how the story progresses between bits of dialogue. Second, he inserts comments about the character or motives of the character. Narration of character is not as common as narration of action. When we see narrator comments about character, we should pay attention as these are crucial to understanding the story. Finally, the narrator from time to time tells us something about God's purpose in the events. These rare narrations of divine intent are like jewels. They give us insight into God's reasons and character.

Anytime you are reading a historical narrative, check first for narration of divine intent. You may want to highlight them. A few examples:

Joshua 4:14	"The Lord exalted Joshua in the sight of all Israel." God desired to grant authority to his leader called to his purpose.
Judges 1:19	"The Lord was with Judah." The reason for Judah's success was not strength but God working behind the scenes.
1 Samuel 2:17	"Thus the sin of the two young men was very great before the Lord." An example is provided of the kind of sin God hates: abuse of authority and privilege.
1 Kings 3:10	"It was pleasing in the sight of the Lord that Solomon had asked this thing." God is pleased when we ask unselfishly for the good of others.
1 Chronicles 11:9	"David became greater and greater, because the Lord of hosts was with him." God's favor can exalt a leader.
Ezra 1:1	"The Lord stirred up the spirit of Cyrus." God can cause people, even non-believers, to do his will.
Ruth 4:13	"The Lord enabled her to conceive." God is in charge of childbirth and conception.

The Basic Theology of the Historical Books

Joshua through 2 Kings, with Ruth left out, is one story, edited in the final version by either one author or a series of authors in succession with the same views on Israel's history. Some scholars call it the Deuteronomistic History because the theology of Deuteronomy is clearly played out in the stories.

That is to say, when Israel obeys, God blesses the land. When Israel disobeys, God allows enemies to torment them, sends plagues, and allows famine.

Central to these books is the concept of God's kingship and human authority. In Joshua, the human leader is Joshua, but it is God who is the warrior king going before his people. God is the one who brings them victory against superior enemies. In Judges, human leaders, often quite imperfect, are God's vessels through whom he rescues Israel at any sign of repentance.

Nonetheless it is God, not Gideon or Samson, who is fighting for Israel. In Samuel, the people want a king for the wrong reason: to better field an army from all the tribes. God lets them have their kind of king, who is a failure. Yet David, who is God's kind of king, submits always to God and brings the land to its greatest blessing. In the books of Kings, all the rulers are judged by how close they come to David's faith and submission.

A special section of the Deuteronomistic history is the long story of Elijah and Elisha. Again, the issue is God's kingship and human authority. Elijah takes on the wicked Ahab with prophetic authority on Mt Carmel in 1 Kings 18. He then offers that authority back to Ahab with a symbolic gesture of running before Ahab's chariot in 1 Kings 18:46. God sent the prophet, a representative of his authority, to straighten out the king. But Ahab would not listen.

So more and more Elijah and especially Elisha replace the king. The many unusual stories of Elisha should be seen in this light.[1] The king is supposed to be the go-to person for help in time of need. Yet the righteous, such as the other prophets and certain righteous Israelites, go to Elisha instead. In fact, when a foreign general, Naaman, needs help, the king is useless and the general must go to the prophet instead.[2] The king has failed as God's representative, so God goes around him completely by using Elisha.

What the Deuteronomistic history (Joshua through 2 Kings) is saying is simple: if Israel would have let God be king, they would never have been destroyed by Assyria and Babylon. Any hope for Israel in the future will be by letting God be the king.

The other historical books have their own unique purposes. Ruth is about righteousness in an unrighteous age. Boaz is an Israelite who blesses his workers by God's name and who obeys the laws of gleaning and levirate marriage.3 The fact that Boaz and Ruth become David's ancestors is a message that God finds righteous people in wicked places.

Esther is unique in that God's name is never mentioned in the story. Esther is like real life. We don't have an inspired narrator telling us what God is doing behind the scenes. It is clearly a miracle of God that Israel is saved from Haman's schemes. The writer deliberately omits God to show us how God works unseen.

Ezra and Nehemiah are about the rebuilding of Judah after the exile in Babylon. They focus on the need for Israel to obey the covenant made through Moses. Ezra is a priest who teaches people the Torah. Nehemiah is a governor who enforces the Torah. Just as Deuteronomy had said, Israel's hope is in obeying God.

Finally, Chronicles takes a unique perspective on Israel's history. The focus is on the positive. The Chronicler is writing after the exile. He calls his people to see the covenant with David and be expectant of the coming Son of David. Whether a human king, or as we now know, a divine Messiah, it is David's heir who will make Israel right again. The Chronicler focuses on worship and the temple as ideals of righteousness.

As much as any other part of the Bible, the historical books point us to God and his ways. By showing more than telling, these stories teach us a deeper lesson. Reading them makes a person of faith want to believe and submit to God's authority.

Chapter Eight
Job, Justice, and Disinterested Love

Many people love the God of Israel in the same way that many pagans loved Marduk, Baal, or Zeus—for his gifts rather than for himself. The problem of Job's day has not disappeared over the millennia. Crowds still gather to seek gifts from God rather than to worship him. Paganism can plague even Christian worship.

Self-centered love is a familiar problem in the sphere of human relationships. When a young man gets married to a much older woman of wealth and means, people are generally suspicious of his motives. Does he love her for who she is or for the lifestyle she can provide?

In a healthy sense of worship, it is reasonable to desire good things from God. In a healthy marriage, both partners bless one another. Likewise, we who worship and love God desire to be blessed. The problem is not the desire but when the desire overtakes worship and service. The problem is when we expect blessing and even demand it. The problem is when God becomes a formula for success.

The Difficulties of Reading Job

The first two chapters and the ending of Job are well known. The vast bulk of the book, from chapter 3 to chapter 42, are less well-known.

Job is advanced poetry. It is not only difficult in English, but is considered the most difficult Hebrew in the Bible. The difficulty in the English, as well as the Hebrew, is that sometimes the poetic imagery is unclear. The poetry is also highly repetitive.

Modern readers tend to have a "get to the point" attitude and resist taking time to enjoy a slowly developed poetic theme.

The structure of the book is vital to understanding its meaning. Job has a prologue and epilogue, a beginning story and an ending story. In between is a long set of poetic dialogues and monologues. There are three rounds of debate between Job and his three friends plus speeches by Elihu and God:

- Ch 1-2 Prologue: Job's Tragedy
- Ch 3 Job's First Speech
- Ch 4-14 The First Round of Debate
  - Ch 4-5 Eliphaz' Argument
  - Ch 6-7 Job's Response to Eliphaz
  - Ch 8 Bildad's Argument
  - Ch 9-10 Job's Response to Bildad
  - Ch 11 Zophar's Argument
  - Ch 12-14 Job's Response to Zophar
- Ch 15-21 Second Round of Debate
  - Ch 15 Eliphaz' Argument
  - Ch 16-17 Job's Response to Eliphaz
  - Ch 18 Bildad's Argument
  - Ch 19 Job's Response to Bildad
  - Ch 20 Zophar's Argument
  - Ch 21 Job's Response to Zophar
- Ch 22-26 Third Round of Debate
  - Ch 22 Eliphaz' Argument
  - Ch 23-24 Job's Response to Eliphaz
  - Ch 25 Bildad's Argument
  - Ch 26 Job's Response to Bildad
- Ch 27-31 Job's Closing Arguments
- Ch 32-37 A Fourth Person Argues (Elihu)
- Ch 38-42:6 God's Case With Job
  - Ch 38-39 God's First Case
  - Ch 40:3-5 Job's First Answer
  - Ch 40:6 – 41 God's Second Case
  - Ch 42:1-6 Job's Repentance and Confession
- Ch 42:7-17 God Restores Job

Satan or the Accuser?

Satan is a character who shows up in only three Old Testament books: 1 Chronicles, Job, and Zechariah.[1] Some interpreters would also see Satan in prophetic passages such as Isaiah 14 and Ezekiel 28, though he is not named.[2]

In Job and Zechariah, Satan is not used as a name but as a title. The Hebrew text should be translated "the Satan" or "the Accuser." Satan is a Hebrew verb meaning to accuse to prosecute. In both Job and Zechariah this is what this supernatural being does. He is an angelic prosecutor and opposes God, as can be seen when God rebukes the Accuser in Zechariah 3.

Some might argue that the accuser in Job could be any angelic being who seeks to discredit God. Yet this is not just any accuser but the Accuser. He is a supernatural being who opposes God and is rebuked by God. The being called Satan in the New Testament is no doubt the same being who accused Job and was allowed to afflict him.

Irony in Job

Irony occurs in a story when the reader knows more than the characters. The reader's superior knowledge often results in situations where the words and actions of the characters mean more to the reader than the characters realize.

In Job, none of the characters, including Job, know why God allowed great tragedies to befall him. Job never learns, even after the fact, that God was using Job as an example to show the angelic beings, especially the Accuser, that there are men who love God purely for the sake of love. The purpose of Job's suffering is God's glory before the heavenly court of angels.

The irony that this leads to is two-fold: Job questions God's justice and Job's friends question Job's righteousness. The reader knows better. God is just and Job is righteous.

The friends imply that Job must have done something to deserve his tragic fate. They are not willing to doubt God's justice and are sure Job must deserve what happened to him. The story of

Job would not work at all if the reader did not know these friends to be completely wrong. Their ironic misunderstanding is the crux of the story.

Likewise, Job's doubt about God's justice is based on his lack of information. Job's situation is just like ours, since we rarely know the reasons behind our suffering. The reader's superior knowledge of God's reasons for his actions inform the story and call on us to keep faith with God during our own suffering.

The Job Triangle

Already we have seen that two issues are debated in Job: the justice of God and the righteousness of Job. There is a third issue which is assumed by both Job and the three friends that completes the picture. The third issue is an idea which has been called the Retribution Principle.[3] This is the idea that God prospers the righteous and causes the wicked to suffer.

The Retribution Principle is generally true but not absolutely true. What I mean is this: it is God's general plan but he has reasons to deviate from it. For example, we have a saying that, "Crime does not pay." It is generally true but not absolutely true. Sometimes criminals get away with their crime and prosper from it, at least for a time. Yet we know that crime almost always carries a heavy price.

In the same way, it is true that God usually delights to help the righteous succeed and prosper while bringing judgment on the wicked. Numerous verses in Proverbs proclaim this:

> The wages of the righteous is life,
> The income of the wicked, punishment.[4]

Yet there are reasons why wicked people get away with their sin, at least for a while. And righteous people suffer for many different reasons. Job is a perfect example of a righteous sufferer.

These three ideas form a sort of triangle:

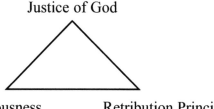

Justice of God

Job's righteousness   Retribution Principle

These are the three ideas in tension in the book of Job and in the debates between Job and his friends. Job is suffering terribly, so the three friends deduce that Job must have sinned to deserve his suffering. Job knows he is innocent and is willing to question God's justice.

What none of the characters consider, but which the unknown author of Job is pointing us to, is that the Retribution Principle is not always true. Many times the righteous suffer and the wicked prosper.

But whose sin is greater: Job's or the friends'? The answer can be seen in Job 42:7:

> It came about after the Lord had spoken these words to Job, that the Lord said to Eliphaz the Temanite, "My wrath is kindled against you and against your two friends, because you have not spoken of Me what is right as My servant Job has."

Job questioned God's justice, which seems a terrible sin. Yet Job repented and was accepted by God. God did not offer the three friends a chance to repent. Their crime was greater than Job's and involved a much greater breach of faith. Their philosophy was, in fact, the pagan philosophy of the day.

The Three Friends as Pagan Philosophers

Ancient Near Eastern religion, in a similar fashion to ancient Greek religion, involved manipulation of the gods. The gods were viewed as man's greatest curse and best hope for blessing. The gods sent famine and feast, plague and health, life and death.

Properly speaking, the gods were not the highest power in the universe. There was a sort of law or force above the gods which we might call magic. Pagan priests used incantations of spells to try to use magic to get the gods to do what they wanted. The gods used magic to control the forces of nature.[5]

From the point of view of the common man, the worship of the gods was to stay out of danger and suffering and to seek blessing. The pagan father wanted many sons born to his wife to carry on his name and he wanted fertile fields. This is why fertility goddesses (Ishtar, Ashtoreth, Aphrodite) and storm gods (Baal, Marduk, Zeus) were the most popular.

When suffering came, a person could go to the temple and pay to have the priests pray to the gods for help. It was assumed that the person had somehow offended the god or goddess. The great hope was that by confessing a broad range of sins and humbling themselves, the worshipper might appease the god. They sought to manipulate the gods into ending suffering and returning blessing.

It did not matter if the worshipper was truly repentant. The gods would not know a person's heart well enough to tell. They were not all-powerful or all-knowing.

In fact, archaeologists found a prayer that was for use in very difficult cases.[6] When all had been tried, if a person could not determine which god had been offended or what the offense was, there was a sort of confession of every sin to every god that could be used:

> May the fury of my lord's heart be quieted toward me.
> May the god who is not known be quieted toward me;
> May the goddess who is not known be quieted toward me.
> May the god whom I know or do not know be quieted
>   toward me;
> May the goddess whom I know or do not know be quieted
>   toward me.[7]

The prayer goes on and on suggesting different possibilities to every imaginable god or goddess confessing unknown sins.

This sort of confession of sin and humbling oneself before the gods is not a matter of repentance, life change, and true worship. It is appeasement or manipulation. Religion is a formula for a better life. The gods are not loved for who they are but only for what they can provide. This is far from the disinterested love that Israel's God seeks.

Job's friends come to him with this standard pagan view of justice, sin, and suffering. Since Job is suffering, he must have sinned. When Job repeatedly and angrily protests his innocence the friends grow angry and think him a liar. Eliphaz, frustrated with Job's denial of guilt and sure that the Retribution Principle is true, starts naming sins Job must have committed:

> Is not your wickedness great, and your iniquities without end? For you have taken pledges of your brothers without cause, and stripped men naked. To the weary you have given no water to drink, and from the hungry you have withheld bread.[8]

What Eliphaz wants Job to do is insincerely confess sins such as these to get God to relent.

Job knows what his friends want and he refuses to lose his integrity:

> Far be it from me that I should declare you right; till I die I will not put away my integrity from me.[9]

Job will not give in to appeasement of God or manipulative religion. He will not say something untrue just to get God to restore him to blessing.

Job knows he is righteous and questions God's justice. The friends know God is just and question Job's righteousness. The author, inspired by God, points us to something else: the reasons for suffering cannot be boiled down to a formula and God cannot be manipulated with insincere prayer. It is the Retribution Principle that should be questioned, not God or Job.

Prosperity Theology and Job

Fast-forward from the days of Job to the present day. Manipulation as religion is still alive and well. One common form of it is prosperity teaching.

Prosperity theology, espoused in many churches especially in America, is the idea that God wants all his followers to be rich and free from disease and suffering. It is remarkably similar to the Retribution Principle:

Retribution Principle	Prosperity Theology
The righteous will prosper and the wicked suffer.	The righteous will be blessed materially and those with weak faith will miss out.

A person dying of cancer is told by well-meaning people, "You don't have to die if you will have faith in God's healing." A person in a wheel-chair comes to a church service to be healed. When it does not happen, people suggest, "You must not have enough faith."

Such people are like Job's comforters. God is a formula for success of you know how to manipulate him. Failures are either swept under the carpet or get blamed on weak faith.

Job is here to teach us a better way. We need not doubt God's justice. We cannot demand blessing. We can believe and accept God's hand without knowing his reasons. We can trust God, who formed the universe and has limitless power, even when we do not understand. One thing we cannot do is manipulate God.

What does God want? What does he delight in with Job before the heavenly court? Disinterested love.

Loving God for Himself

Disinterested love does not mean loving without emotion or interest in the person. It means loving without self-interest. It means loving the person for who he or she really is.

Job had disinterested love. When everything was taken from him, Job would not curse God. He said, "The Lord gave and the Lord has taken away."[10] When his wife demanded that Job curse God he rebuked her saying, "Shall we indeed accept good from God and not accept adversity?"[11]

Job is pointing us to true religion. It is not about manipulating God with insincere prayer and seeking the gift. It is about viewing all of life as under God's dominion and loving him without self-interest. It is about loving the Giver even if he takes away the gift.

Chapter Nine
Psalms as Israel's Prayerbook

I once heard a pastor say something like this, "Jesus never meant for us to literally pray the Lord's Prayer but only to use it as a model for our own prayers." He went on to say that God would not want us mindlessly repeating words and calling it prayer.

Many believers do pray the Lord's Prayer. Many pray the Psalms. Many pray words that are written in prayer books or devotional books.

Yet many others have a prejudice against praying pre-written prayers, which can be called liturgical prayers when used in a public worship service. The thinking goes like this, "If you recite words written on a page instead of praying from your own thoughts, you will just be mouthing words and not meaning them from the heart."

On the other hand, those who love praying the Psalms, the Lord's Prayer, and other scriptures and prayers, might put it differently. They might say, "If you only pray spontaneously you are usually just giving God your clumsy thoughts and missing out on beautiful scriptural and traditional thoughts of prayer that carry you to greater heights."

The truth is, the Bible evidences both kinds of prayer. Moses and other leaders of the Bible prayed in their own words. Yet the Bible also contains many prayers intended for use by the congregation of Israel and the disciples of Jesus. A well-rounded life of worship and prayer will include both spontaneous and liturgical prayer. Those who only pray spontaneously miss out some great theology and poetic expression in prayer. Those who only pray liturgically miss out on personal expression.

The rabbis, who passed down a lengthy prayer-book for Judaism (mostly using verses from the Psalms and Prophets) emphasize devotion when reciting prayers. It is not true that praying in someone else's words or even praying the same words every day leads to mindless repetition. Sometimes familiarity with the words leads to deeper meditation. Always using Biblical prayers reminds us of God's priorities.

The Psalms are the prayer-book and hymnal of Israel. To fail to pray the Psalms is ignoring part of God's word. To merely read them and not use them in worship and prayer is a shameful waste.

Psalms can be read in Bible studies and worship services to focus the group on God and his Word. Psalms can be prayed in private devotion. Psalms can be read prayerfully and silently or out loud to God. The Psalms contain the most beautiful thoughts about God in the Bible. The Psalms are also filled with great theology for those who know how to read them.

Psalm 1 and 2—The Foundation of the Psalter

Psalm 1 is about the Torah, God's commandments and instructions for his people. Psalm 2 is about the Messiah. Torah and Messiah, the revelation of God and the salvation of God—these are the building blocks of our entire faith.

We do not know who finally arranged the Psalms and put them in order. There are five books of the Psalms just as there are five books of Moses (1-41, 42-72, 73-89, 90-106, and 107-150). Many are by David, Asaph, and the Sons of Korah, who all lived around the same time. Yet others are anonymous. Some are clearly during and possibly after Judah's exile in Babylon. Someone put them together in a certain order and most likely with a reason and purpose in mind.

It is not hard to imagine why Psalm 1 and 2 come at the beginning. They set the stage for what the Psalter is about. They are prayers and songs of faith—faith in God, his Word, and his Messiah.

Psalm 1 is a contrast, about two kinds of people:

The Righteous	The Wicked
Do not walk in the ways advised by the unrighteous.	Advise people to walk selfishly.
Delight in God's commandments.	Scoff at God's revelation.
Are healthy like trees planted by water.	Are dying like the dry chaff that comes off of wheat.
Yield fruit and prosper.	Will be found guilty at the judgment and perish.

The message sent by placing this Psalm at the beginning of the Psalter is simple. The Psalms are for those who seek after God and delight in his commandments. The Psalms are a book for the righteous. The Psalms are in perfect agreement with the law of Moses.

Psalm 2 is slightly more complex and introduces several themes common in the Psalms:

The nations	The Gentile nations, who usually oppose Israel, are under God's authority though they do not know it.
God's throne	God sits in heaven, meaning that he rules the earth unseen.
God's king	This is David and his descendants who were given a covenant. But ultimately this is Messiah, the one who will come from David's line.
The Son of God	Although it is true that Jesus is "God the Son," the title "Son of God" does not mean that. It is a title for the Davidic kings and the Messiah. It comes from 2 Samuel 7:14.

To better understand the concept of Messiah and how it relates to King David, see chapter 14.

In Psalm 2, God's universal rule centered on the Davidic King, and ultimately Messiah, is made known. The nations of the earth have their own schemes for domination and expansion, but it is God's kingdom and God's King that will triumph.

The Torah and the Messiah are right at the beginning of Psalms. The prayers and theology that follow all relate to God's revelation and salvation.

Types of Psalms

There are three basic kinds of Psalms: praise, lament, and wisdom.[1] Some others divide Psalms into categories by ways they may have been used: temple entrance liturgy, hymns, individual laments, corporate laments, thanksgiving psalms, royal psalms, and wisdom psalms.[2]

Both ways of looking at the Psalms can be helpful:

Praise	Often start with a command such as "Sing" or "Praise."	Examples: 8, 29, 30, 33, 34, 66, 104, 111, 113, 116, 138.
Lament	Often start with direct address such as "Oh Lord."	Examples: 6, 12, 13, 31, 39, 44, 74, 79.
Wisdom	Less common. These address some issue of wisdom.	Examples: 1, 32, 37, 49, 119.

Praises in the Psalms can be divided into two types: descriptive and declarative.[3] Descriptive praise says something about God while declarative praise states the intention of the speaker to praise or thanks God for something he has done.

Lament Psalms follow a pretty regular pattern:[4]

Complaint	Petition	Declaration of Faith	Vow to Praise

The lament Psalms are a wonderful example of how honest we can be with God in prayer.

The Psalms can also be more specifically categorized as follows:[5]

Type	Characteristics	Examples
Temple Entrance	Used probably as songs or prayers when pilgrims came into the temple.	15, 24
Hymns	Start with command to praise, describe God's goodness, and conclude with command to praise.	136, 145
Individual Lament	Start with direct address, complaint, petition, declaration of faith, and end with vow to praise.	13
Corporate Lament	Similar to individual but they address a situation affecting the nation. Sometimes are more negative than individual laments. Often refer to past saving deeds for the nation.	80
Thanksgiving Psalms	Start with personal praise, recount a saving act of God, a vow of praise, and a command to praise.	30
Royal Psalms	Deal with Davidic King and/or Messiah.	2, 45, 72, 110.
Wisdom Psalms	Teach about God and his Word.	1, 32, 34, 37, 49, 119.

Special Collections of Psalms

The Psalms are divided into five books. Yet within the five books of the Psalms there are collections of Psalms grouped by author or theme:[6]

- Davidic Group I: 3-41.
- Sons of Korah Collection I: 42-49.
- Davidic Group II: 51-65.
- Asaph Group: 73-83.
- Sons of Korah Collection II: 84-88.
- Hymns Collection I: 95-100.
- Hallelujah Collection: 111-117.
- Songs of Ascent to Jerusalem: 120-134.
- Davidic Group III: 138-145.
- Hymns Collection II: 146-150.

How to Pray the Psalms

We don't have the opportunity at present to go to Jerusalem with the throng of worshippers at the temple and see the Psalms used in all their grandeur. One day we will be at that great dance in Zion, with the throng rejoicing before Messiah Jesus and chanting Psalms as we approach the Holy City. For now, the Psalms can be used in private prayer and worship as well as in public worship services.

Not every Psalm is fitting for every need and situation. In a time of praise, for example, it would not be fitting to read a lament. When there is distress and suffering, a lament may be better suited to the occasion. Wisdom and Royal Psalms are best suited for teaching and proclaiming truth about God.

The very first prayer in the book of Psalms, Psalm 3, is a lament. You might not think that's how it would be. Praise seems more spiritual than lament, or at least we think so. You'd expect the first prayer in Psalms to be praise, and high praise at that.

Lament is a fancy way to say complaint. To lament is to mourn aloud, to wail, to express sorrow or regret. That's what

David does in the very first prayer of the Psalms: "O Lord, how my adversaries have increased!"

Psalm 3 is a prayer about adversaries, foes, enemies, betrayal, problems. Why would the first prayer be about enemies and problems?

The answer tells us something about the nature of Psalms. They are not poems but prayers. They are not about beauty so much as honesty.

The first time I saw the movie *Fiddler on the Roof*, I was shocked by scenes where Tevye the milkman talks to God. One day he is bringing his milk cart home. The Sabbath is about to start. He is going to be late for the Sabbath because his horse got a sore foot. He complains to God in very honest words. "Isn't it enough I am poor? Do you have to hurt my horse too?"

But Psalms are like that. In Psalm 42:9, the writer asks God, "Why have you forgotten me?" Do you feel like praying that to God sometimes? Why not pray it?

The Psalms give us permission to pray to God with honesty. They are not all laments, however. There are numerous praises in the Psalms. And even the laments end with praise. David includes in Psalm 3 a declaration of faith: "I will not be afraid of ten thousands of people." He ends with praise, "Salvation belongs to the Lord." This is the way to bring your faith to resolve your complaint.

To pray the Psalms, simply take the voice of the speaker and say the words to God from your heart. It helps to make this a habit and read and pray the Psalms frequently. Make notes in your Bible of favorites for different situations. Your prayer life will never be the same.

And it helps to remember as you pray: your voice is joining myriads of others now and in the past. Many Israelites, including Jesus, prayed these words. When you pray them, you join your prayers with theirs and your prayer is much bigger than yourself. You are praying God's own words back to him!

Chapter Ten
Wisdom, Doubt, and God

We are all pilgrims in this world. We travel through life with limited knowledge of our surroundings and with only a few tools to get by.

A traveler walking to Jerusalem to meet with God passes through unfamiliar territory. Life is like that unfamiliar territory. On our way to God through the turns, rises, and drops of existence we cannot know what to expect next. The calm can be shattered at any time or it can continue. The traveler needs to be prepared in advance.

Of all the tools God has given his pilgrims to make it through this troubled world, the most practical is wisdom. The best way to walk an unfamiliar road is with someone who knows it well.

God raised up wise men who shared with us wisdom about the turns, sudden drops, and obstacles of the road. The Wisdom Literature of the Bible—Job, Proverbs, Wisdom Psalms, Ecclesiastes, and Song of Songs—makes the Torah practical and useful for walking.

The Torah tells us what to believe and how to live. The Wisdom writings tell us how to apply that teaching when the road gets difficult.

Wisdom supports Torah. Solomon says, "Where there is no vision, the people are unrestrained, but happy is he who keeps the law [Torah]."[1] The teaching of God, especially in Genesis through Deuteronomy, is the vision that keeps our lives going. Proverbs promises to help the pilgrim of faith put that vision where the sandals hit the road.

Experiencing Proverbs

In the Torah the pilgrim was asked to believe and obey. Now, in Wisdom, the pilgrim is asked to think. To live is to ask questions and sometimes find answers.

Wisdom promises us, if we only knew its value, we would seek it above all things. We would be willing to read and ponder it every day.

The traveler seeking God starts in Genesis with creation and goes on to read of Sinai, sanctuary, and sacrifice. The faith of one God over all things is made plain. The pilgrim continues into the history of Israel where experience and Torah begin to meet. Israel experienced a simple pattern. When they followed Torah they were blessed and when they departed from it they were pressed on all sides by hateful enemies, fear, and starvation. Wisdom concurs, saying, "The way of the Lord is a stronghold to the upright, but ruin to the workers of iniquity."[2]

Then the traveler crosses from history into the Wisdom writings. At the beginning of Proverbs he finds a promise of practical help for the road tomorrow and the day after:

> The proverbs of Solomon the son of David, king of Israel: To know wisdom and instruction, to discern the sayings of understanding, to receive instruction in wise behavior, righteousness, justice and equity; to give prudence to the naive, to the youth knowledge and discretion, a wise man will hear and increase in learning, and a man of understanding will acquire wise counsel, to understand a proverb and a figure, the words of the wise and their riddles.[3]

Already in this introduction is a chest of priceless information for those who take the time to ponder its meaning.

This introduction has three specific lessons for the needy pilgrim:

1. To understand what proverbs are.
2. To know how to become wise.
3. To know eight words for wisdom and knowledge.

The traveler on God's road of faith is about to experience help for the journey.

What is a Proverb?

The proverbs in Hebrew are *mishlei* from the word *mashal*. Properly speaking, a *mashal* is a simile.[4] In case you forgot your grammar school education, a simile is a comparison using the word "like" or "as."

Many of the proverbs are similes. This is a basic form of wisdom saying:

> Doing wickedness is like sport to a fool... (Prov. 10:23).
> As a ring of gold in a swine's snout, so is a beautiful woman who lacks discretion (11:22).
> The way of the lazy is as a hedge of thorns (Prov. 15:19).

The comparison and contrast of the proverbs is generally where their wisdom lies. Proverbs 10:23 tells us that evil is like a game to a foolish person. The second half of the proverb goes on to say that a wise person makes a game out of wisdom instead.

Life is full of comparisons and contrasts. Being wise is about know what things go together and what things do not. It is about knowing how to order our world so that we follow the good and reject the bad.

Solomon has given us *mishlei*, proverbs, to help us compare and contrast the things that matter and the things that hinder the good life God wants us to live.

The first lesson for the pilgrim is to pay attention to the comparisons and contrasts of the similes that we call the Proverbs.

How to Become Wise

The first six verses of Proverbs tell us how to become wise. They use eight verbs which give us the path from ignorance to wisdom:

To know	First we must know the sayings by reading them.
To discern	Second, we must interpret them.
To receive	We must be willing to receive what they say.
To give	We are helped in our wisdom by teaching it to others.
To hear	We have to listen or we won't learn.
To increase	We need a goal of increasing knowledge and never being satisfied.
To acquire	We need to think of learning wisdom as acquiring wealth for our lives.
To understand	Then we will understand.

In other words, to become wise we must make Wisdom a pursuit, a study, a hobby.

This may sound simple, but few people do it. Few people will read Proverbs regularly and observe life for examples of Proverbs in action. Few people will teach their children Proverbs or study it with a friend or spouse. Few people think of wisdom as wealth for living.

To become wise, you must want it. The benefit will be less pain, less mistakes, a closer relationship with God, and a closer relationship with people. Wisdom promises all these things.

Have you ever been in a class where you barely paid attention? Maybe you doodled on your paper or fell asleep drooling in class. You just couldn't bear to listen as the teacher droned on and on, when, all of a sudden, the teacher called your name and asked you a question.

It is easy to miss a lot in life by not paying attention. Life gives no warning when all of a sudden you are expected to know what to do and how to react. It is easy to miss wisdom.

You don't want to be doodling, or worse yet, drooling,

when God calls your name! Be ready. Know, discern, receive, give, hear, acquire, and understand so that God will give you a better life.

Eight Words for Wisdom and Knowledge

The first six verses of Proverbs also teach us eight words for wisdom that better help us to understand what it is and why we should seek it:

Wisdom	Wisdom, *khokhma*, is skill at life, learning how to order it and succeed.
Instruction	Instruction, *moosar*, can come the easy way or the hard way. The easy way is study. The hard way is bad experiences that discipline us to learn better.
Understanding	Understanding, *beenah*, is related to the word for "between." It is about seeing distinctions between one thing and another. This is a life-skill.
Wise behavior	*Seykhel* is also known as common sense, or applying wisdom to action.
Prudence	*Ormah* is also known as craftiness, which can be good or bad. The serpent in the Garden was crafty in a bad way. Yet Jesus commanded us to be as crafty as serpents. It means having a plan.
Knowledge	*Da'at* is a general word and comes through study and observation.
Discretion	*Mezimah* is a lot like *ormah*. It is about planning and succeeding.
Learning	*Lekakh* is related to the word for acquiring. The wise learn and do not lose what they learn. They acquire it like wealth.

The Topics of Proverbs

The book of Proverbs could be seen as having three sections:

1. Chapters 1-9: Sermons or discourses on wisdom, its value, and its relation to God.
2. Chapters 10-29: Individual proverbial sayings on various topics. These sayings are not grouped together, but are collected almost randomly.
3. Chapters 30-31: Wisdom sayings and discourses from Agur and Lemuel.

In Proverbs 1-9, Solomon is like an evangelist. He has read the wisdom of the world and invites Israel and the outside world also to come and pursue wisdom with him. Solomon used wisdom as a way to draw people to God.

In the main section of Proverbs, however, it is as if we are reading Solomon's collection without any organizing principle. Perhaps he wrote them all in a scroll and never arranged them by topic.

This is good for the reader. It makes reading Proverbs an adventure. One verse might be about the dangers of words and the next about pride. Each proverb is a surprise, an adventure.

Yet it is also good for the reader to know the topics of Proverbs and to have examples.5 Proverbs can be seen as having eighteen basic topics:

1. The Righteous and the Wicked. Examples: 10:16, 24, 25; 11:5-6, 18; 12:3; 13:21; 14:26, 32; 19:16; 28:1, 4, 9.
2. Wisdom and Folly. Examples: 10:1, 19; 11:12; 12:23; 13:14; 14:1; 15:24; 16:23; 17:21, 25, 28; 18:2, 6, 15; 19:8; 21:16; 24:3-4; 27:12; 29:11, 20.
3. The Tongue and Its Consequences. Examples: 10:14, 32; 11:9; 12:14, 18; 13:3; 14:3; 18:2, 13, 21; 21:23; 29:5, 20.
4. Family Relationships. Examples: 14:1; 15:20; 17:6; 18:22; 19:26; 20:20; 22:6; 23:15-16, 26; 25:24; 27:8.
5. Anger and Strife. Examples: 10:12; 14:17; 15:1; 16:32; 17:1, 9, 14, 27; 19:11, 19; 21:19; 26:17; 27:15-16.

6. Humility. Examples: 11:2; 12:9; 15:25; 16:18, 19; 18:12; 22:4; 25:6-7; 27:1, 2, 21.

7. Love and Kindness. Examples: 11:17; 12:25; 14:21, 31; 17:17; 18:24; 20:6; 21:21; 22:9; 24:17-18; 25:21-22; 28:27.

8. Authority. Examples: 16:12, 13; 17:26; 18:5; 21:1; 28:15; 29:4, 26.

9. Honesty and Justice. Examples: 11:20; 12:17, 22; 13:6; 14:5, 25; 19:1, 5, 9, 28; 20:17; 21:6; 28:6.

10. Discipline and Reproof. Examples: 10:17; 12:1; 13:13, 18, 24; 15:10, 31, 32; 19:20; 20:30; 21:11; 22:15; 23:13-14; 27:5, 6; 28:23; 29:17.

11. Finances. Examples: 11:24-26; 19:17; 22:7; 27:23-27; 28:27.

12. The Lord. Examples: 10:27, 29; 14:26-27; 15:11, 26, 29; 16:2, 5, 9, 33; 17:3, 15; 18:10; 19:21, 23; 20:10, 24, 27; 21:31; 29:25.

13. Laziness and Diligence. Examples: 10:4, 5; 12:11, 24, 27; 13:4; 14:4, 23; 20:13; 22:13; 24:27.

14. Self-Control and Excess. Examples: 20:1; 23:20, 21.

15. Poverty and Wealth. Examples: 10:22; 11:4; 15:16-17; 16:8, 19; 19:1.

16. Reputation and Gossip. Examples: 18:8; 25:8-10.

17. Counsel and Forethought. Examples: 12:15; 15:22; 19:20; 21:30.

18. Joy and Sadness. Examples: 14:10, 13, 30; 15:13, 30; 18:14; 25:20.

Dealing with Doubt: Ecclesiastes

Every pilgrim on the way to Jerusalem is going to encounter doubt. Where is God when the righteous suffer and the wicked prosper? Can I believe in God in the face of death? Doesn't it all just seem meaningless? Why is God silent?

Many people think Ecclesiastes is depressing. Like Job, Ecclesiastes deals with the subject of doubts and problems with

God's justice in the world. Yet Ecclesiastes is not depressing, but liberating if read properly.

Sometimes people say Ecclesiastes was true only before Jesus came. Before Jesus came, some would say, life was meaningless. But now that Jesus has come, life is fulfilling.

This is also not true. Jesus has not yet redeemed the world. Ecclesiastes is still very much true. In fact, Paul sounds an awful lot like the writer of Ecclesiastes when he says:

> For the creation was subjected to futility, not willingly, but because of Him who subjected it, in hope that the creation itself also will be set free from its slavery to corruption into the freedom of the glory of the children of God. For we know that the whole creation groans and suffers the pains of childbirth together until now.[6]

The English translation "futility" is a synonym for the word that Ecclesiastes uses to describe the world: vanity.

The key to understanding Ecclesiastes is to know that the author, probably Solomon, is breaking you down to liberate you and build you back up. He is trying to liberate you from foolish expectations of fulfillment in this life.

Some people read Ecclesiastes as if it is saying, "Eat and drink for tomorrow you die." Yet this is not a balanced reading of the book. The Preacher of Ecclesiastes balances faith with an honest look at doubt:

The Downside of Life	The Advantage of Faith
"All is vanity" 1:2.	"This also I have seen, that [enjoyment] is from the hand of God" 2:24.
"There was no profit under the sun" 2:11.	"God has made everything appropriate in its time" 3:11. "Remember also your

"And how the wise man and the fool alike die!" 2:16.	Creator in the days of your youth" 12:1.
"For who knows what is good for a man during his lifetime?" 6:12.	"The conclusion, when all has been heard, is this: fear God and keep his commandments" 12:13.

What the Preacher is telling us is simple and as true as ever: there is no fulfillment in life but there is God. It is foolish to expect lasting fulfillment in success, wealth, learning, love, or any other pursuit. Rather, we should enjoy the simple pleasures of life (2:24-26; 3:12-13, 22; 5:18-20; 8:15; 9:7-9), to eat and drink and see the good in our labor. Meanwhile we should put all hope of fulfillment in God alone.

The Preacher did not have a clear view of the afterlife, since God revealed it late in Biblical history.7 He put his hope in God and considered it a mystery how God would bring the fulfillment that this life lacks.

We need this perspective, because we still put our hopes in foolish things. Most of the things we trust in are mere band-aids on the hurt of life. A vacation disappoints. A romance fails. Our hope can only be in God and then we can enjoy simple pleasures and leave ultimate meaning and purpose to him. This way of looking at life will liberate us from foolish optimism and make realistic experience easier to bear.

Romantic Love: Song of Songs

Every pilgrim on the way to Jerusalem is going to encounter romantic love, for good or bad. God did not leave this controversial subject out of the Bible. In fact, in what may seem a scandal to some, he includes graphic sexual poetry in the Bible.

Some people cannot accept Song of Songs, also called Song of Solomon, at face value. It seems beneath God to give us a series of erotic poems. Therefore, it has been a longstanding tradition to interpret Song of Songs as an allegory. Some of the best writings of Christian history have been allegorical interpretations of the Song. Typically the Song is taken as a love poem between God and his people. The sexual imagery is not about human love, but about God and man's passionate relationship to each other.

Yet it is better to take the Bible at face-value and not find hidden meanings with no basis in reality.

Another mistake in reading the Song of Songs is to try and make one story out of all the poems in it. Many commentaries seek to find a set of characters in a drama. There are two main dramas proposed. In one Solomon and a young maiden fall in love and Solomon pursues her. In another, a young shepherd falls in love with a maiden and wicked Solomon tries to steal her away.

Both the allegorical and dramatic readings of Song of Songs run into numerous contradictions and problems. It is better to take the book as it is: a collection of erotic poems organized around a proverb about the joy and peril of romantic love.

The main point of Song of Songs is found in 8:6-7:

> For love is as strong as death, jealousy is as severe as Sheol; its flashes are flashes of fire, the very flame of the Lord. Many waters cannot quench love, nor will rivers overflow it; if a man were to give all the riches of his house for love, it would be utterly despised.

Here we find, back top back, two proverbs about love that could just as well be included in the book of Proverbs. Instead they are located in the middle of a series of poems about romantic love.

The poems illustrate the power and danger of love, which is exactly what the proverbs are about. Love is as strong as death. Many have died for romantic love and it will keep on happening. Romantic love is a human emotion more powerful than any other. This is good and bad.

It is good because it can be a great joy. It is bad because it can ruin our lives. The wise pilgrim headed for Jerusalem will take this proverb into account and regard romance as dangerous, yet greatly to be desired in its appropriate context.

Chapter Eleven

Four Prophetic Parts

If Israel is known for anything, it is known for monotheism, Sabbath, and...prophets.

Fiery orators delivering messages of judgment for sin and instruction for righteousness, the prophets of Israel are the successors of Moses. Moses said, "The Lord your God will raise up for you a prophet like me from among you, from your countrymen, you shall listen to him."[1]

Impassioned orators like Amos cried out, "Let justice roll down like waters And righteousness like an ever-flowing stream."[2] Fearsome prophets of judgment like Jeremiah decried the sin of their generations, "Where are your gods which you made for yourself? Let them arise if they can save you."[3]

At times the prophets were gentle, teaching those who believed the prophetic word how to know God, "What does the Lord require of you but to do justice, to love kindness, and to walk humbly with your God?"[4]

Sometimes the prophets would sing, perhaps even dance, as they declared future hope for Israel and Judah, "Shout for joy, O daughter of Zion! Shout in triumph, O Israel! Rejoice and exult with all your heart, O daughter of Jerusalem! The Lord has taken away His judgments against you, He has cleared away your enemies. The King of Israel, the Lord, is in your midst; you will fear disaster no more."[5]

Yet, in spite of their fiery oration and joyful promises for the days of Messiah, the prophets are often thought of as boring reading. For the most part, this perception is caused by a lack of understanding.

Four Parts: The Key to Reading the Prophets

We are often bored by what we do not understand. If we do not know what to look for in a collection of words then it is no more than that: a collection of words.

The writings of the prophets are not all prophecy. The prophets also contain history and poetry. Some prophetic books are mostly history, such as Jonah. The first key to reading the prophets is being able to tell the difference.

Yet it is in the prophecies themselves that modern readers typically need the most help. When Isaiah speaks doom, saying, "Woe to the rebellious children who execute a plan, but not mine,"[6] many feel a yawn already coming on. And then Isaiah goes on, describing a group who are going down to Egypt against the word of the Lord. How can this apply to my life, a reader wonders.

The prophets have a gloom and doom reputation. And there is gloom and doom in the prophets. It can be depressing to read. But that is not all that is in the prophets. Nor is the gloom and doom irrelevant.

In order to understand the prophets it is important to know the four kinds of prophetic messages they deliver:[7]

1. Judgment: announcing in advance disasters and consequences for specific sins.
2. Allegation: naming the sins of Israel and Judah that will lead to judgment.
3. Instruction: God's teaching to the people about how to avoid judgment and turn back to him.
4. Future Hope: promises of days when Israel and Judah will be restored and revived.

What bores many readers of the prophets are lengthy prophecies of judgment and allegation.

The judgments and allegations of the prophets become less boring when each prophet and their historical period is better understood.

Understanding the Times of the Prophets
There are sixteen books of prophets. Four are considered major, not meaning that their words are more important, but that they are longer books: Isaiah, Jeremiah, Ezekiel, and Daniel. Twelve are called the minor prophets, because their books are shorter and, in ancient times, they could all be written on one scroll.

The prophets are not printed in chronological order in our Bibles. Those who try to read them without knowing their times are at a disadvantage.

To better understand the times of the prophets, it is necessary to know of two terrible historic events. In 722 B.C.E. the Northern ten tribes of Israel were destroyed by Assyria. In 586 B.C.E. the Southern kingdom of Judah was destroyed and Jerusalem razed. The following chart puts the prophets in their context:

Isaiah	740-700 B.C.E. Isaiah wrote chapters 1-39 to his own generation, warning of a coming invasion by Babylon. He wrote chapters 40-66 to future generations who would return from Babylon.	This is the most Messianic of all the prophets (see chapter 14 about Messianic Prophecy). Isaiah wrote mostly warnings in the first half of his book and mostly comfort and promise in the second half.
Jeremiah	625-586 B.C.E. Jeremiah is often gloomy, forced to warn his people about the coming destruction by Babylon. In 586, Babylon completely destroyed Jerusalem as Jeremiah had warned.	Jeremiah was a depressed prophet, forced to deliver terrible news to his people, who regarded him as a traitor. He also, however, soars to heights of future hope and Messianic prophecy.
Ezekiel	593-571 B.C.E. This prophet wrote from Babylon, warning	Ezekiel is a difficult, but rewarding, prophet to study. His

	those in Jerusalem of the coming destruction. His visions of God's glory and of the Messianic temple are complex and powerful.	judgments are strong, but he has a great deal of future hope material. The last nine chapters describe in detail the temple to be built in the days of Messiah.
Daniel	605-539 B.C.E. Daniel is history combined with visions. He was in Babylon explaining the times and kingdoms that would rise, leading to Messiah's kingdom.	Many commentaries suggest Daniel is fiction written much later. He describes kingdoms one after another leading to Messiah's kingdom. He foretells many specific details of Israel's future that are now history. His predictions seem too accurate to some, so they suggest his writings are from after the events.
Hosea	753-722 B.C.E. in the Northern Kingdom of Israel. Hosea foretold the Assyrian destruction of Israel in 722.	Hosea warned the ten tribes of Israel until destruction came in 722. He also foretold future hope for Israel.
Joel	Unknown time period.	Joel warns of a locust plague and a day of the Lord. He also warns of the ultimate Day of the Lord, the final events of this age of the world. He describes Armageddon in detail.

Amos	760-750 B.C.E. to the Northern tribes of Israel though he was from Judah.	He too warned of the coming destruction in 722. His focus was on the reasons for the coming judgment, especially social injustice. He also made great promises of future hope and a Messianic Age.
Obadiah	Probably 586 B.C.E.	A short judgment on Edom for siding with Babylon against Judah.
Jonah	Probably before 750 B.C.E.	Mostly history, this book is the remarkable adventure of a prophet in Ninevah, the city that would destroy Israel in 722 B.C.E. It is a warning to Israel to repent, as even the Assyrians were willing to repent when God foretold judgment.
Micah	740-700 B.C.E. A contemporary of Isaiah. Micah 4:1-3 is the same as Isaiah 2:2-4.	Micah especially warns the corrupt leaders of Judah. His book contains remarkable prophecies of the birth of Messiah, kingdom of Messiah, and Judah's future restoration.
Nahum	Sometime before 612 B.C.E.	This short prophecy is God's judgment

		against Assyria for destroying Israel. Ninevah fell in 612.
Habakkuk	Approximately 640-626 B.C.E.	Habakkuk saw the coming destruction by Babylon and considered the justice of God. He concluded in the end that even if God let Judah be destroyed, God was to be worshipped.
Zephaniah	Approximately 626 B.C.E. At the start of Jeremiah's career.	Zephaniah warned the people well in advance that Babylon would destroy them. He also beautifully promises of future hope at the end of this short book.
Haggai	520 B.C.E. After the return from Babylon.	Haggai was a prophet after the exile in Babylon. He encouraged the people to finish building the temple and he encouraged the post-exilic leader, Zerubbabel.
Zechariah	520-518 B.C.E. Also after the return from Babylon.	This complex prophet called for revival, temple completion, and hope in the post-exilic leadership. Zechariah is also a book of Messianic prophecies, including prophecies about the

		triumphal entry, the suffering and return of Messiah, and his kingdom. Chapter 14 details Armageddon and the kingdom of Messiah.
Malachi	Somewhere between 515 and 458 B.C.E. This was a period of spiritual decline between the temple's rebuilding and the reforms of Nehemiah and Ezra.	Malachi is a post-exilic prophet calling for revival. His book details the issues of sin in his time. The end of Malachi moves into future hope, reminds the people to keep the law of Moses, and foretells the return of Elijah.

How to Read the Prophets

Once the reader knows what to look for in the prophets and understands their location in time, reading them becomes much easier.

The prophets are primarily composed of the first two types of prophecy: judgment and allegation. Rare but worth their weight in precious gems are the passages of instruction, where God tells the people how to change and how to live. Slightly more common, but also less than common, are the beautiful promises of future hope.

When reading the prophecies of the Bible (remember not all the writing in the prophetic books is prophecy) it is important to keep the four types of prophecies in mind. The following set of rules for reading will greatly help:

1. Read the verses in question and determine if they are judgment, allegation, instruction, or future hope.
2. Determine where the section you are reading begins and

ends. Look for changes in subject matter (could be in a few verses or after a whole chapter).

3. Determine how a judgment or allegation fits into a time period. Who is being blamed for what and what are the consequences?

4. Determine how God's judgments and allegations apply to modern readers. Are we guilty of similar sins?

5. If the passage is instruction, determine how God's teaching applies to your life. What changes should you make?

6. If the passage is future hope, has it already happened or is it still a future hope for Israel and for God's followers? These promises should not be taken away from Israel and considered promises for the church (that is bad interpretation). Yet the church will enjoy the benefits of God restoring Israel and Judah and bringing Messiah to rule the world from Jerusalem.

To help make this reading process easier, we will look at an example from Isaiah. Also, chapters 12 and 13 will detail the message of the prophets that we are labeling instruction and future hope.

Example: Isaiah 1:16 – 2:4
I chose this passage because in short space it contains all four types of prophecy:

1. Judgment.
2. Allegation.
3. Instruction.
4. Future Hope.

Before reading and understanding a passage, it is necessary to locate it in time and situation. To understand Isaiah 1:16 – 2:4, we must remember that Isaiah was writing to Judah in 740 B.C.E. and warning them of a coming destruction by Babylon that would not happen for a century and a half.

Reading Isaiah 1:16 – 2:4, it is quickly apparent that this passage begins with instruction. God is telling the people what to do:

- Make yourselves clean (1:16).
- Cease to do evil (1:16).
- Learn to do good (1:17).
- Seek justice, especially for the defenseless (1:17).
- Your sins can be white as snow (1:18).
- If you obey, you will be forgiven (1:19)
- If you rebel, you will be devoured (1:20).

So our first section for this passage is Isaiah 1:16-20. It consists of God's instruction to Judah for revival to prevent destruction.

Starting in verse 21, we can see we have moved into allegation. God is charging the people with sin and naming their sins:

- The city has become a harlot and refuge of murderers (1:21).
- Your silver has become dross (1:22).
- Your rulers are rebels (1:23).
- People love bribes (1:23).
- The defenseless are not being protected (1:23).

So our second section is 1:21-23 and it is about allegation. These are the reasons Judah will be judged unless they repent.

Moving into verse 24, God begins announcing judgment:

- I will avenge myself on my foes (1:24).
- I will turn my hand against you (1:25).
- I will smelt away your dross (1:25).

The judgment is short-lived and then God begins making promises. So our third section is 1:24-25 and it is judgment.

Then God begins giving the people future hope:

- I will restore your judges (1:26).
- Zion (Jerusalem) will be redeemed (1:27).
- The repentant ones will be righteous (1:27).

So our fourth section is 1:26-27 and it is about future hope.

Then God turns back to the sinners and returns to judgment:

- Transgressors will be crushed (1:28).
- Sinners will be embarrassed on that day that they made shrines under oak trees to foreign gods (1:29).
- Since you worshipped under a tree, you will be like a tree whose leaves are falling off (1:30).
- You will burn like dry wood (1:31).

The fifth section, then, is 1:28-31, which is a strong judgment.

The next section begins at 2:1, with an introductory formula in verse 1. The prophecy itself begins in verse 2 and is clearly future hope:

- In the last days (2:2).
- The mountain of the house of the Lord (temple) will be raised up (2:2).
- Nations (Gentiles) will come to the temple (2:2).
- Gentiles will say, "Let's go worship God in Jerusalem" (2:3).
- Gentiles will desire to learn the law of God (the Torah) (2:3).
- God will judge the world righteously (2:4).
- They will hammer swords into plowshares (2:4).

The final section is a surprising message of future hope in which Israel will become the center of a world revival. Combining this with other prophecies will lead to the simple conclusion that these events will take place after Messiah returns.

So, to review our passage, here is what we have found:

- 1:16-20 Instruction—do good and find forgiveness from God.
- 1:21-23 Allegation—you have lost righteousness and are not protecting the defenseless.

- 1:24-25 Judgment—you will suffer but not be eliminated.
- 1:26-27 Future hope—you will have your leadership restored and be redeemed.
- 1:28-31 Judgment—but those who do not repent will be destroyed like the trees under which they worship idols.
- 2:2-4 Future hope—one day Jerusalem will be the center of world revival, peace, and the teaching of the law of Moses.

There is much to apply to our lives, as modern readers, from these verses:

1. God desires righteousness and wants to forgive us for our sins if we will listen.
2. God does not allow us to decline into spiritual apathy without consequences.
3. God desires that we help the defenseless.
4. God abhors us allowing anything to come before him in priority, which is idolatry.
5. Though times may get bad, the last word will be God's and the faithful will enjoy a future of peace and God's rule over earth from Jerusalem.

Boring? Hardly. The prophets do not deserve their reputation. We simply need to learn how to read them and apply their precious insight to our own lives.

Chapter Twelve

Render Your Hearts
and Not Your Garments

Sometimes the prophets did not speak judgment or allegation. Sometimes God gave them a message of instruction, some teaching for the people about how to change their lives.

A true-to-life example can be found in the ancient book of Joel. Joel is a prophetic book whose location in time cannot be made definite. Joel gives no specifics that would tie his book to a specific period.

Imagine living in an age without grocery stores and public water. Imagine living in the hills of Judah, a land only a few inches of rain away from being a desert. Imagine having enough food in good years, but easily going into famine when there is a drought. This is the situation in which Joel lived and prophesied.

The people had been living with inadequate rain and inadequate crops. This was not merely a matter of inflated prices of grain. This was a matter of strict rationing of grain. The elderly and often the children would die during such times.

Then, to make matters worse, enormous clouds of locusts descended on the fields, eating entire crops. The weary, starving citizens noted various species of locusts coming in different years and seasons. They gave them different names, but one after another they took away the little the people had left.

Joel felt his people's agony and God gave him a message meant to drive the people to their knees in humble prayer for God's rescue. Joel said to them, "Wail like a virgin in sackcloth,"[1] a heart-rending image of an unmarried young woman bereaved of her betrothed.

Things About to Get Worse

Then Joel delivers a terrifying message. Things will get worse. "Blow a trumpet in Zion."[2] The trumpet is a warning of an approaching army. Only this army is not made up of marauding soldiers, but winged terrors flying in colossal swarms to destroy stalk and leaf.

Joel calls this approaching plague of locusts the "day of the Lord."[3] That is, this will be the day of the Lord's judgment on his people. In perhaps the most poetic passage, Joel says the land before the locusts looks like the Garden of Eden, but the land behind them looks like a desert.[4]

The people believe in gods and goddesses. The God of Israel is one of many gods they take to be real. The people of Israel and Judah have a history of rejecting the monotheism they have taught the world.

From their pagan point of view, this terrifying announcement calls for standard measures. The people might tear their clothes and put on sackcloth and make an outward show of being humbled in hopes God, or the gods, might relent.

Joel's Powerful Instruction from God

God sends Joel a clear word. Joel, as always in prophecy, receives exact words from God. Joel's people are on the edge of devastation. What will God say?

"Yet even now," declares the Lord, "Return to Me with all your heart, and with fasting, weeping and mourning; and rend your heart and not your garments." Now return to the Lord your God, for He is gracious and compassionate, slow to anger, abounding in lovingkindness and relenting of evil. Who knows whether He will not turn and relent and leave a blessing behind Him, even a grain offering and a drink offering for the Lord your God? Blow a trumpet in Zion, consecrate a fast, proclaim a solemn assembly, gather the people, sanctify the congregation, assemble the elders, gather the children and the nursing infants. Let the bridegroom come out of his room and the bride out of her bridal chamber. Let the priests, the Lord's ministers, weep between the porch and the altar, and let them say, "Spare Your people, O Lord, and do not make Your inheritance a reproach, a byword among the nations. Why should they among the peoples say, 'Where is their God?'" Then the Lord will be zealous for His land and will have pity on His people.[5]

God will not accept ritual repentance such as tearing clothes. God will accept the tearing of an old, unrepentant heart. God will accept true life change and repentance.

After all, God is quick to forgive and slow to anger. The people's idolatry was ever before him and God acted slowly to judge. He gave his people many warnings and much time to repent. That time, however, was running out.

In this prophecy, Joel is not judging or making allegations. He is bringing God's message of life-change to the people. He is preaching what might be called the gospel of his day.

For Then or Now?

So are Joel's words, "rend your hearts and not your garments," out of date? Has the sacrifice of Messiah, the death of Jesus for our sins, made Joel's message obsolete for today?

Absolutely not. First, it is evident that modern followers of God suffer the same maladies as Israel and Judah. People are still given to show over substance. That hasn't changed.

Our lives suffer as a consequence of our rebellious attitudes and actions. Occasionally something difficult happens in a way that we can clearly connect with our sin.

A job is threatened by our selfishness, laziness, territorial spirit, pride, or lack of team effort. A marriage is threatened by our addiction to pornography, participation in an affair, or a controlling, manipulative spirit. A friend is lost through our rudeness.

Whatever it may be, sometimes we see direct consequences from our sin.

Yet few of us get at the root. In such a case, hopefully our faith causes us to feel miserable at our sin. What do we do with the misery?

One solution can be likened to a band-aid. We go for counseling about the pornography addiction hoping to appease an injured spouse. We have no intention of really stopping. It is the fact that we are going to counseling that we hope will satisfy the spouse and save the marriage.

Another solution can be likened to surgery. We submit ourselves to God and say, "Heal us because we can't stand to go on this way." We get to the heart and ask God to expose inner layers. We rend our hearts, exposing them to heaven and asking for cleansing within.

This is not a formula or a set of steps to sinless perfection. We do not become instantly holy. But we open ourselves to God and if the sin creeps up again, we do it all over again. We find our holiness increasing in stages.

All this from a few simple words from God: rend your hearts and not your garments.

What Are Your Multiplied Sacrifices to Me?

There is a large strain of prophetic teaching about heart-repentance and soul-obedience versus empty ritual and religious posturing.

Before examining these biblical texts in some detail, it is important at the outset to avoid a common, tragic mistake. Many people will read God's words against empty ritual and conclude that ritual is bad.

For example, in the first century, the Romans viciously destroyed Jerusalem and the temple of God in its midst. Judaism was a temple-centered religion. Even Jews living in other countries thought of the temple, and the sacrifices and prayers offered there, as their covering.

Without a temple, how could the Jewish people go on with their calling to be priests to the world? How would their faith in God continue?

A rabbi and leading scholar named Yokhanan ben Zakkai had the answer. He read Hosea 6:6 where God says, "I delight in loyalty rather than sacrifice." The sage replied that the Jewish people needed loyal devotion to God and not sacrifices.[6]

Someone might agree saying, "That's true since the sacrifices merely pointed to Jesus and had no value of their own." In a larger sense, someone might say, "Rituals don't matter at all. We need a faith devoid of rituals."

But look deeper at the prophets and you will see many holes in this type of thinking. God is not against rituals. He prescribed many rituals in the Old and New Testament. Rituals properly understood and practiced have great value. Rituals mandated directly in scripture and rituals practiced as tradition in God-fearing communities have great value.

Consider for example one of the greatest examples of the prophetic teaching about ritual versus reality:

When you come to appear before Me, who requires of you this trampling of My courts? Bring your worthless offerings no longer, incense is an abomination to Me. New moon and sabbath, the calling of assemblies-- I cannot endure iniquity and the solemn assembly. I hate your new moon festivals and your appointed feasts, they have become a burden to Me; I am weary of bearing them. So when you spread out your hands in prayer, I will hide My eyes from you; yes, even though you multiply prayers, I will not listen. Your hands are covered with blood.[7]

At first we might be tempted to say that God never really liked the sacrifices on the altar at the temple or the Sabbaths and festivals of Israel. God asks, "Who required these?"

As we think about it, we realize, "But you required them God." We wonder, "How can God say these are wrong when he commanded them?"

Reading further down the passage, we see God saying the same thing about prayer as he said about sacrifices and festivals. Is God against prayer? No, there must be some other answer.

To Obey is Better than Sacrifice

If we become avid readers and fast learners about the Bible, we will find that numerous prophetic teachings make a similar point. In fact, the first prophet to make this point in a stunning way was Samuel.

Saul was a king who had a shallow view of God. Like most other people in the Ancient Near East, he saw God as a means to blessing instead of as a sovereign Lord. Saul was given victories by the Lord, but he did not completely follow God's instructions. He spared the livestock of his enemies thinking to offer them as a great sacrifice to God. What a ceremony it would be and what a great gift to God it would be, the king thought. Yet God had told him not to spare their livestock.

So Samuel came down to the battlefield and to the foolish king. He demanded to know why God's instructions had not been followed. Saul explained about the sacrifice.

Samuel delivered a message God had given him the previous night in a dream. The essence of Samuel's message came in 1 Samuel 15:22:

> Has the Lord as much delight in burnt offerings and sacrifices as in obeying the voice of the Lord? Behold, to obey is better than sacrifice.

God wants obedience more than sacrifice was the clear message.

From the time Samuel delivered this message until the end of the Old Testament, it is repeated again and again in various forms:

1 Samuel 15:22	To obey is better than sacrifice.
Isaiah 1:12-15	Your Sabbaths, festivals, and prayer are an abomination to me.
Jeremiah 7:9-10	Will you steal and murder and then come and stand before me?
Hosea 6:6	I delight in loyalty rather than sacrifice.
Amos 5:21-24	I hate your festivals...take away from me the noise of your songs.
Psalm 40:6-8	Sacrifice and meal offering you have not desired...I delight to do your will.
Psalm 51:16-17	You do not delight in sacrifice...the sacrifices of God are a broken spirit and contrite heart.

Here is what the prophets are saying. God is not against the sacrifices that he commanded. He is not against Sabbaths and festivals which he commanded Israel. He is not against prayer.

God is against empty sacrifices, empty Sabbath-keeping, empty festivals, and prayer without repentance and obedience.

God could just as easily deliver a message to our generation saying: "Who asked you to sing these hymns and songs? Who requires this meaningless worship you offer me? Who asked you to give your money and build these buildings in my name? Who requires these prayers you offer to me? Who asked you to baptize and take the Lord's Supper?"

God wants loyalty, true devotion, not money, songs, and prayers. With repentance, devotion, and obedience, songs and prayers means a great deal. Ceremonies and rituals mean a great deal when offered with devotion by obedient followers. But even the largest gift, the longest prayer, and the most beautiful service of communion is offensive to God when we are not living the truth on the inside that we profess on the outside.

Seek Good, Justice, and Righteousness

The prophets offer instruction for us that is as beautiful and practical today as it was over 2,500 years ago. The gems of instruction in the prophets are rare, buried in larger chapters of judgment, allegation, and future hope. They are gemstones worth finding and pulling out.

For example, Isaiah goes on to say in 1:16, "Wash yourselves, make yourselves clean." We need to be reminded that repentance starts with us determining to change our lives. Then Isaiah takes us to God in verse 18, "Come now, and let us reason together . . . though your sins are as scarlet, they will be white as snow." Repentance begins with our desire to change and ends with God bringing forgiveness.

A famous piece of prophetic instruction, which was called to mind by Martin Luther King, Jr. in his speeches about civil rights, is from Amos 5:24:

> Let justice roll down like waters and righteousness like
> an ever-flowing stream.

Anyone reading Amos can see what he means by justice. He means that a society must treat everyone with goodness and equity. If we treat the poor and defenseless badly, then we are guilty of injustice and we invite the wrath of God.

In the instruction of the prophets, we find that living God's way is not about being religious. If we have the outward trappings of religion but we lack love and real action to help those around us, our words are empty to God. If we do obey God's commandments and reach out to help others, then our songs, prayers, and rituals are filled with meaning. They must work together. This is what the prophets are trying to tell us.

Chapter Thirteen

Every Man a Vine and Fig Tree

The prophets of Israel and Judah delivered four kinds of messages to the people: judgment, allegation, instruction, and future hope. It is in regard to the future hope passages that we must address a major interpretive issue that plagues us.

When people read in the prophets about great days ahead when Israel will be restored and the land will become a paradise and Jerusalem will be made great, it is tempting to imagine ourselves as the direct recipients of these promises. Typical thinking might go like this, "This is God's promise to his people. Back then his people were Israel. Today his people are the church."

There is an understandable desire to make scripture relevant and directly applicable. Sometimes to make a scripture more relevant we ignore its context. Even well-meaning people who interpret the Bible literally are guilty of this. We want to find what will preach rather than what it means. So, people who are not Jewish wear T-Shirts proclaiming:

> 'I know the plans that I have for you,' declares the Lord, 'plans for welfare and not for calamity to give you a future and a hope.'[1]

The problem is that these verses were spoken to the people of Judah. To take this promise away from Judah and apply it to yourself is like stealing.

Supersessionism

Many people apply God's promises to Israel to themselves or to the church without thinking deeply about why they do it. Others do it intentionally. A certain philosophy of Bible interpretation developed quickly in the days of the apostolic fathers and the church fathers that continues to this day.[2]

Theologians use the word supersessionism to describe this philosophy of interpretation. A more popular word for it is replacement theology.

The idea of supersessionism is that the church supersedes Israel as God's people. A simple case can be made as follows:

1. God promised Israel a Messiah.
2. Messiah came.
3. Israel largely rejected the Messiah.
4. Many Gentiles, now forming the church, accepted him in Israel's place.
5. God has removed his promises from Israel and given them to the church.

Based on this interpretation, Israel is no longer God's people and the promises made to them are either fulfilled already, transferred to the church, or they will simply never be fulfilled.

There are numerous scriptural issues and problems with supersessionism. We will make a simple case here that God's promises are still for the Jewish people. More detailed considerations can be found in "Appendix A: Are God's Promises Still for the Jewish People?".

It is important to understand the future hope prophecies of the Bible as being literally for Israel. I hope to settle this issue quite simply in the minds of the readers with two verses from Romans:

God has not rejected his people whom he foreknew.[3]

The gifts and calling of God are irrevocable.[4]

We find from Romans that Israel is still God's Chosen People and that God has not revoked his gifts or calling to Israel. (See Appendix A for more).

Fitting Old Testament Hope into a View of the End Times

There are various views about the end times. It is beyond the scope of this book to consider in depth the options and rationale for the various views. Yet, whatever view of the end times you hold, the Old Testament promises Israel a time of restoration, with Messiah in the midst of the nation and the temple rebuilt.

This vision of a restored Israel, of Jesus ruling from the temple rebuilt in Jerusalem, and of Old Testament festivals and worship being practiced, seems difficult for some Christians to reconcile with their faith. It would seem that the temple worship and festivals are the old way and our new way is better. Hopefully, the chapters in this book about the sacrifices and the temple have dispelled some of those ways of thinking.

The three major Christian views of the end times are:

1. Pre-Millennialism: Jesus will return and rule from Jerusalem for a thousand years and then the New Earth will be formed forever.
2. Post-Millennialism: The church will penetrate the whole world and bring peace for a thousand years and then Jesus and the New Earth will come forever.
3. Amillennialism: Jesus is already ruling from heaven for a time comparable to a thousand years and he will return and establish the New Earth forever.

Of these three views, only one leaves room for the Old Testament prophecies of future hope to be fulfilled as they are written. Only pre-millennialism has an interim period of 1,000 years centered in Israel before the New Earth. Therefore, in the following glimpse at the Old Testament hope, we will follow a pre-millennial model. Many of the prophecies of future hope to Israel would seem to find their fulfillment in the millennial reign of Messiah Jesus.

The World to Come, as Described by the Prophets

At long last the heir from the broken line of King David will come to Jerusalem.[5] He will establish his rule over the earth, a dominion that will never end.[6]

He will return at a specific place, on the Mount of Olives outside Jerusalem. He will come at a time of great war, with the armies of the world attacking Jerusalem. His feet will split the mountain in half and the Jewish survivors will escape through the valley he creates.[7] The king will slay the armies attacking Jerusalem and establish his rule of peace over the nations.

The hearts of all Israel will be made new,[8] circumcised,[9] and filled with the law of Moses.[10] The king will rule from the temple in Jerusalem, larger and more glorious than the previous temples of God. The nations of the world will come to the temple in Jerusalem to learn the law.[11] They will also come annually to celebrate the Feast of Booths.[12]

Swords will be made into plowshares and the world will know incredible peace.[13] The land of Israel will become a paradise, with the desert blossoming.[14] A river of life will flow from the temple and make the Dead Sea alive.[15] Trees will grow by the river whose leaves are for healing.[16] Agriculture in Israel will be so easy that the ones planting will not finish before the harvesters catch up to them in the fields.[17]

Other nations are specifically mentioned for blessing in the days of Messiah. Egypt and Assyria will be as godly as Israel.[18] Iran will be restored in the last days as well.[19]

People will live long lives, being thought sickly if they die at one hundred.[20] But wait, you ask, what about us? What about those who lived and died before the days of Messiah?

We will be there too. The Old Testament teaches resurrection of the dead as early as Isaiah 26:19, "Your dead will live; their corpses will rise. You who lie in the dust, awake and shout for joy." Daniel 12:2 adds that, "Many of those who sleep in the dust of the ground will awake, these to everlasting life."

It is the New Testament that completes the picture and helps us see where the resurrection of the dead and the restoration of Israel intersect. 1 Thessalonians 4 says the dead whose faith was in Messiah Jesus will rise first. The living believers at his return will rise next. This will happen at or before the return of Messiah. Revelation 20:4-5 says that the believers in Messiah will be raised before the millennium and the rest after it.

But what about Israel? What will become of the Jewish people enduring and surviving the tribulation of the last days? They will all be saved, as it says in Romans 11:26. The kingdom of Messiah will be filled with Jewish and Gentile believers from the ages, even those from Old Testament times.

So if we are resurrected, we won't die again. But Isaiah says in the days of Messiah a person who dies at the age of one hundred will be thought young. How can these be reconciled?

Putting the New Testament facts together with the Old Testament facts, we can answer that question. Those who believed in Messiah before his return will be resurrected before the millennium. The survivors of the nations who were not believers will enter the millennium unresurrected. They will still be mortal. Those who become followers of Messiah during the millennium will not be raised until the end.

This is the picture given in the Old Testament prophecies of future hope. Israel will be the center of the world. Jesus, the heir of David's throne, will rule from Jerusalem. It is a beautiful picture of a better time. Several of the many prophecies of future hope deserve a closer look.

New Hearts

Ezekiel is often thought dry by those who fail to understand his magnificent prophecy. The beauty of Ezekiel can be seen in many places, not least of which in 36:24-28:

> For I will take you from the nations, gather you from all the lands and bring you into your own land. Then I will sprinkle clean water on you, and you will be clean; I will cleanse you from all your filthiness and from all your idols. Moreover, I will give you a new heart and put a

new spirit within you; and I will remove the heart of stone from your flesh and give you a heart of flesh. I will put My Spirit within you and cause you to walk in My statutes, and you will be careful to observe My ordinances. You will live in the land that I gave to your forefathers; so you will be My people, and I will be your God.

First Ezekiel foretold a day when Jewish people would be called back from every nation into Israel. This regathering of Israel is echoed from Moses' great prophecy in Deuteronomy 30:1-6. Jeremiah 23:7-8 says this regathering will surpass the exodus.

Second, Ezekiel describes Israel as being made clean. God will bring the people to forgiveness by converting their hearts.

Third, and related to the second, Israel will receive new hearts. This is close to the image of Deuteronomy 30:6, where Israel's hearts are circumcised. The new heart will not be stubborn like stone, but responsive like flesh.

Fourth, God will implant his Spirit. As we know from the New Testament, the third person of the Trinity, the Holy Spirit, dwells inside believers. This had not yet happened in Ezekiel's day and the prophecy is remarkable.[21]

Fifth, and unnoticed by many interpreters who see no continuing place for the law of Moses, God will cause Israel to follow the statutes. What statutes could he be talking about? God calls them "my statutes," which should lead us to ask: what statutes belonged to God in Ezekiel's time? The answer is simple: the statutes of Moses. The law, far from being abolished, will still be followed in the days of Messiah.

Finally, Israel will live in the land. This ought to confirm that Ezekiel's prophecy is for an interim period, before the New Earth spoken of in Revelation 21-22. Like many other future hope prophecies, Ezekiel 36 is about the millennium, the kingdom of Messiah based in literal Israel.

The New Covenant

Jeremiah 31:31-34 is often misunderstood. It seems evident from the sayings of Jesus that the New Covenant is already here.[22] So many interpreters assume the New Covenant is roughly equivalent to the gospel or to the New Testament. This is incorrect.

"Behold, days are coming," declares the Lord, "when I will make a new covenant with the house of Israel and with the house of Judah, not like the covenant which I made with their fathers in the day I took them by the hand to bring them out of the land of Egypt, My covenant which they broke, although I was a husband to them," declares the Lord. "But this is the covenant which I will make with the house of Israel after those days," declares the Lord, "I will put My law within them and on their heart I will write it; and I will be their God, and they shall be My people. They will not teach again, each man his neighbor and each man his brother, saying, 'Know the Lord,' for they will all know Me, from the least of them to the greatest of them," declares the Lord, "for I will forgive their iniquity, and their sin I will remember no more."

Consider the promises of the New Covenant:

• It is with Judah and Israel (Gentiles are not mentioned).
• It is unlike the Sinai Covenant.
• Yet it still has the same law as the Sinai Covenant, only written on hearts.
• No one in the world will need to be taught about God since all will know him.
• There will be forgiveness for sin.

This is certainly not a prophecy that has been fulfilled. We still have to teach people about God since most of the world does not know him.

So what did Jesus mean when he equated his death with the New Covenant in Luke 22:20? He meant that the New Covenant had begun, not that it was complete yet.

We do see the New Covenant started. There is forgiveness of sin for those who know God and believe in Messiah. Gentiles, not mentioned in Jeremiah, are included as co-heirs with Israel. The rest of the promise is waiting for the Age to Come.

So the New Covenant is not the gospel and it is not the New Testament. It is a promise to Israel for the future. In the New Testament we see that Gentiles will also receive the blessings of the New Covenant. It is now, for us who believe, and not yet, for the whole world.

Vines, Fig Trees, and Sweet Wine

It sounds odd to modern people. Imagine if your vision of heaven was being able to sit under your own vine and fig tree. Yet for those living in a semi-arid climate with rocky soil and torturous ravines and hills, this was not a bad vision of paradise at all.

In the days of Solomon, the land was at peace and had prosperity. So it was said that Israel had "every man under his vine and fig tree."[23] A spokesman for Assyria cried out to the terrified inhabitants of Jerusalem that if they would only surrender, Assyria would allow them all to sit under their vine and fig tree.[24]

Micah 4:1-3 describes Jerusalem restored, the temple rebuilt, and the nations coming to learn the law on Mt Zion. Then Micah 4:4 describes Jewish paradise:

> Each of them will sit under his vine and under his fig tree, with no one to make them afraid, for the mouth of the Lord of hosts has spoken.

Agricultural paradise is common in the prophecies of future hope.

Joel 3:18 promises sweet wine dripping from the mountains. Isaiah 25:6 describes God throwing a banquet on the mountains of Israel with aged wine. Amos 9:13 describes the harvest taking so long they will still be treading grapes when it is time to prepare the next season's crop.

In the Talmud, a book of Jewish tradition and interpretation, the rabbis speculated fancifully about the nature of Israel in the days of Messiah:

> Not like this world is the World to Come. In this world one has the trouble to harvest the grapes and to press them; but in the World to Come a person will bring a single grape in a wagon or a ship, store it in the corner of his house, and draw from it enough wine to fill a large flagon, and its stalk will be used as fuel under the pot. There will not be a grape that will not yield thirty measures of wine.[25]

In the days of Messiah, the curse of Genesis 3:17-18 will be lifted. The ground will easily produce for us and the land will be filled with figs, grapes, and wine.

Zechariah 3:10 takes the promise one step further. The vine and fig tree are not only a sign of peace and prosperity, but of friendship and community:

> 'In that day,' declares the Lord of hosts, 'every one of you will invite his neighbor to sit under his vine and under his fig tree.'

Paradise was originally a garden according to Genesis. In fact, the very word paradise is a Persian loanword used in the Bible. In its original form it means a garden. We started in a Garden and God is taking us back to a Garden. That's paradise.

A Quick List of Some of God's Future Hope Prophecies

The following list is not complete, but should be an aid to you in further study. Most of the concepts introduced in this chapter are referenced in the following list. Studying the future hope prophecies is studying about heaven on earth. These are among the most comforting scriptures in the Bible. When combined with truths from the New Testament, they truly give a full picture of the Age of Messiah:

1. Jerusalem and the temple will be established (Isaiah 2:2-4; Micah 4:1-3).
2. Gentile nations will make annual pilgrimage to Jerusalem to the temple (Isaiah 2:2-4; Micah 4:1-3).
3. The law will be taught to the world from Jerusalem (Isaiah 2:2-4; Micah 4:1-3).
4. The remnant of Israel will be the pride of all the earth (Isaiah 4:2-3).
5. God will cover Jerusalem with a bridal canopy and his glory will shine as in the wilderness (Isaiah 4:5).
6. Messiah will reign from David's throne in Jerusalem forever (Isaiah 9:7).
7. Israel will be regathered from every nation to the land (Deuteronomy 30:1-6; Isaiah 11:11-12; Jeremiah 23:7-8; Ezekiel 36:24; Zechariah 10:8-12).
8. Egypt and Assyria will be as godly as Israel (Isaiah 19:23-25).
9. The Judean desert will become a flowering paradise (Isaiah 35:1-2).
10. The nations will bring offerings to the temple (Isaiah 60).
11. Some Gentiles will be chosen to serve with the priests in the temple (Isaiah 66:20-21).
12. Gentile nations will keep the biblical Sabbath (Isaiah 66:23).
13. The regathering of Israel in the last days will surpass the exodus (Jeremiah 23:7-8).
14. In the New Covenant the law is not abolished but written on hearts (Jeremiah 31:33).
15. The Levitical priests will continue to function (Jeremiah 33:18).

16. God will give new hearts to regathered Israel and place his Spirit in them (Ezekiel 36:24-27).
17. Israel will continue keeping the statutes of Moses (Ezekiel 36:27).
18. The temple will be rebuilt larger than ever (Ezekiel 40-48).
19. There will again be sacrifices in the temple (Ezekiel 43).
20. There will be festivals as in the law of Moses (Ezekiel 45:21-25).
21. A river of life will flow from God's temple (Ezekiel 47).

Chapter Fourteen

The Messiah in the Old Testament

One of the glorious discoveries every reader of the Old Testament makes are the Messianic prophecies. Jesus is foretold in the Hebrew scriptures. How joyful the disciples on the road to Emmaus must have been when "He opened their minds to understand the Scriptures, and He said to them, 'Thus it is written, that the Messiah would suffer and rise again from the dead the third day.'"[1]

Yet many people are disappointed that there are not more clear references to Messiah, and especially to the cross. They are there, to be sure. But it has happened over the centuries that people have over-done Messianic prophecy. Wanting there to be more, many have found Messianic prophecies where they do not exist.

It is an important principle that Bible texts mean what they were intended to communicate to their original audience. Finding secret or hidden meanings in the Bible is counter to God's plan to reveal himself to people through the Bible.

Therefore, in this presentation of Messiah in the Old Testament, we will only look at solid Messianic prophecies. If some of your favorites (Psalm 22 or Isaiah 7:14, for example) are not listed or discussed here, it is because many of these are better interpreted in other ways.

What we want to know is this: what does the Bible say with authority about the Messiah?

Messiah As a Word

Most English Bibles rarely or never use the word Messiah. That is because Messiah is not the only translation possible for that word. Let's consider the literal meaning of the word, Messiah.

Messiah is a coined word from the Hebrew moshiakh, which means anointed. Most people do not use the word anointed on a daily basis and are unaware of its meaning.

In the Ancient Near East, when a person became a king, prophet, or priest, there was often a ceremony of anointing. Anointing is a physical ceremony involving oil, often perfumed oil, being poured over the head of the person being inaugurated.

How much oil would be poured? Well, Psalm 133 makes a reference to the anointing ceremony of Aaron, the first high priest. The Psalm says, "It is like the precious oil upon the head, coming down upon the beard, even Aaron's beard, coming down upon the edge of his robes."[2] This was no thimble-full of oil or a smear on the forehead. It was a shower of oil over the head.

In the ancient world, fragrant oil was used for personal hygiene. In an age with less bathing and no deodorant products, fragrant oil refreshed and cleansed. The person being inaugurated into high office was anointed perhaps as a way of making them pure.

In the Old Testament, the same word that means Messiah is often used in verb form for anointing. Also, any person ordained to high office of king, priest, or prophet may be spoken of as "an anointed" or "the anointed." We could say of them that they were "a messiah." Examples include Saul, David, and even the pagan king Cyrus.[3]

Yet an idea developed in Israel of a coming Anointed One who would surpass David and Aaron and all other anointed ones. This is what we think of when we speak of Messiah.

The Messiah Concept

By the time of Jesus, various groups in Israel were expecting various types of Messiahs. Some expected more than one Messiah. For example, some expected a great Prophet Messiah, Priest Messiah, and King Messiah.

It was the King Messiah concept that caught most people's imagination. There were false Messiahs. Craig Evans lists more than a dozen false Messiahs just from the 1st and 2nd centuries.[4]

Why were the Jewish people of Jesus' day so bent on seeing the coming of Messiah? Who was this Messiah and why did they expect him?

The answer begins with what is perhaps the most important of all the Messianic Prophecies and certainly the foundation of the concept: 2 Samuel 7:12-16:

> When your days are complete and you lie down with your fathers, I will raise up your descendant after you, who will come forth from you, and I will establish his kingdom. He shall build a house for My name, and I will establish the throne of his kingdom forever. I will be a father to him and he will be a son to Me; when he commits iniquity, I will correct him with the rod of men and the strokes of the sons of men, but My lovingkindness shall not depart from him, as I took it away from Saul, whom I removed from before you. Your house and your kingdom shall endure before Me forever; your throne shall be established forever.

God spoke this promise to David. Specifically God promised David in these verses:

- An unending line of heirs to sit on the throne of Israel.
- That he would be a father to David's heirs, making them sons of God.
- That the line of David would last forever.

What do you do when one of God's promises seems to fail? That is exactly what happened. David's line continued for about 400 years. There were good and bad kings in his line. But God did not let his line fail, until the Babylonians came, starting in 605

B.C.E. Then the last king of David's line was taken captive into Babylon. David's line was ended.

It might seem that God's promise had failed. But the believers waited. They assumed that God would restore David's line quickly. When the survivors of Judah returned from Babylon, they were led by Zerubbabel, David's heir.[5] Would he be the one to restore David's throne? Would he be the son of God for his generation?

No, Zerubbabel was only allowed to be governor. He did not take the throne. Judah had no king. Had God's promise failed?

That leads us to a second great Messianic Prophecy, a Psalm that reasserts God's promise and calls on God to fulfill his promise: Psalm 89. In verses 38-42, the Psalm complains:

> But You have cast off and rejected, You have been full of wrath against Your anointed. You have spurned the covenant of Your servant; You have profaned his crown in the dust. You have broken down all his walls; You have brought his strongholds to ruin. All who pass along the way plunder him; He has become a reproach to his neighbors. You have exalted the right hand of his adversaries; You have made all his enemies rejoice.

As Psalm 89 declares, God is supposed to bring an heir to David's throne. And so Israel waited. Israel waited for more than 500 years.

And then we come to the time of Jesus. After waiting more than 500 years, what was Israel's situation in Jesus' time? They were under Roman rule. And the Romans, who were not bad rulers compared to many other empires, were hard on the Jewish people. And the people wanted out from under the thumb of Rome. And they spoke of a Messiah, an anointed one from David's line, who would restore Israel and defeat Rome.

And the people who believed in this Messiah who would set them free had plenty of scripture to back up their belief.

Numerous prophecies about a Messiah-figure declared that he would defeat the armies of the nations and make peace in the world.

From the time that Zerubbabel did not become the Messiah, the people waited. Zechariah, the prophet from Zerubbabel's generation, drove the people even more to look for Messiah to come. In the days when the people hoped Zerubbabel would ascend, Zechariah said:

> Rejoice greatly, O daughter of Zion! Shout in triumph, O daughter of Jerusalem! Behold, your king is coming to you; He is just and endowed with salvation, Humble, and mounted on a donkey, Even on a colt, the foal of a donkey.[6]

Types of Messianic Prophecies

In this treatment of Messiah in the Old Testament, we are only concerned with prophecies whose literal meaning points to a Messianic leader or a Messianic Age. And within this group of prophecies, there are several types:

- Prophecies of a Messianic Age, focusing on the times and conditions more than the person.
- Indirect Messianic Prophecies, speaking of David's line or the seed of Abraham, but not getting specific about Messiah.
- Prophecies of King Messiah, focusing on the second coming of Jesus as King.
- Prophecies of the Suffering Messiah, focusing on the first coming of Jesus.

It is important to say that we are presenting here the New Testament view of the Messianic prophecies. In Judaism there are some differences since, other than in Messianic Judaism, Jesus is not regarded as the Messiah. Some Bible scholars will dispute Jesus being identified with some of these prophecies on other grounds. Yet for those who know that Jesus is the fulfillment of the Old Testament, we can easily see how these prophecies point to him.

Listing the Messianic Prophecies

The following lists, except for the first category, are intended to be relatively complete. Many other authors would include more references, but the ones included here are literally about Messiah and do not involve hidden meanings or allegories.

The Messianic Age

See chapter 13 for more details on the Messianic Age. These prophecies refer more to the times and conditions of the days of Messiah than to the person of Messiah. The following list is very incomplete and intended to provide a few examples of numerous prophecies:

- Isaiah 2:2-4 (Micah 4:1-3).
- Jeremiah 23:5-8.
- Jeremiah 31:31-34.
- Ezekiel 36:24-28.
- Ezekiel 40-48.
- Daniel 2:44-45.
- Daniel 7:13-14.
- Joel 3:18-21.
- Amos 9:11-15.
- Micah 4:4-8.
- Zephaniah 3:12-20.
- Zechariah 14:1-4, 16-21.

Indirect Messianic Prophecies

- Genesis 22:18 (Abraham's seed).
- Genesis 49:10 (Judah's scepter).
- Numbers 24:17-19 (The Star of Jacob).
- 2 Samuel 7:12-18 (The Son of God).
- Psalm 2 (The Anointed Son).

- Psalm 89 (The Davidic King).
- Psalm 110 (The Priest like Melchizedek).
- Amos 9:11 (The Fallen Booth of David).
- Micah 2:12-13 (The King who Breaks).

Prophecies of King Messiah
- Hosea 3:5 (David, their King).
- Micah 5:1-4 (A Ruler from of Old).
- Isaiah 9:1-7 (Light of Galilee, Prince of Peace).
- Isaiah 11:1-16 (Root of Jesse, Righteous Judge).
- Isaiah 61:1-3 (Healer of the Broken-Hearted).
- Jeremiah 23:5-6 (Branch of David).
- Jeremiah 30:21 (The Leader in the Last Days).
- Jeremiah 33:14-26 (Branch of David).
- Ezekiel 21:25-27 (The One to whom it Belongs).
- Ezekiel 34:23-21 (The One Shepherd).
- Ezekiel 37:24-28 (David, my Servant).
- Daniel 7:13-14 (Son of Man).
- Zechariah 9:9-10 (The King on a Donkey).

Prophecies of a Suffering Messiah
- Isaiah 42:1-4 (The Gentle Servant).
- Isaiah 49:1-7 (The Servant's Despair).
- Isaiah 52:13—53:12 (The Suffering Servant).
- Daniel 9:25-26 (The Anointed One Cut Off).
- Zechariah 12:10 (The Pierced One).

The Two Strands of Messianic Prophecy

If I speak to a religious Jewish person about Jesus being Messiah, I often hear the objection, "Then why isn't there world peace?" This objection sounds strange to the ears of many of Jesus' followers who are so used to assuming that Messiah had to suffer and die.

But how clearly understood was the suffering of Messiah before the death of Jesus? To find the answer, simply look at the disciples. The disciples of Jesus were good Jews with a decent amount of biblical knowledge. They understood the words of the prophets as well as most people in their day.

When Jesus told Peter he would die, Peter said, "God forbid it, Lord! This shall never happen to You."[7] If it was hard for Peter to understand, should we be surprised when God's Chosen People today do not understand? Can we not represent Jesus to Jewish people with more understanding and respect if we understand what the Old Testament really says about Messiah?

To a religious Jewish person, Messiah is the one who restores Israel and brings peace to the world. This is true. But the Old Testament says more. The Old Testament has two strands of Messianic prophecy: King Messiah and Suffering Messiah.

How can these two things be reconciled? How can the same person destroy the armies of nations and bring peace to the world on the one hand and yet be "like a lamb is led to the slaughter"[8] on the other hand?

It is the New Testament, not the Old Testament, that provides the answer. Jesus came the first time to be a sacrifice for sin, as Isaiah 53 so clearly declares.[9] But he will come back and fulfill all the prophecies of King Messiah. He will not be the lamb when he returns, but the Lion of Judah.

Appendix A

Are God's Promises Still for the Jewish People?

In chapter 13 we introduced the concept of supersessionism, the idea that the church has superseded Israel as God's people. This point of view is also called replacement theology (the church has replaced Israel in God's plan).

Those who accept the doctrine of supersessionism cannot take the future hope prophecies of the Bible at face value. As we showed in chapter 13, God's promises to Israel and Judah are very specific and show that the Age to Come is based in Jerusalem. God's future hope prophecies involve an Israel-centered and very Jewish kingdom of Messiah coming at the return of Jesus.

Long books have been written about this subject, which we are going to treat briefly here. It is my hope in a few pages, to thoroughly persuade you that supersessionism is not the truth of God's Word.

Those who hold to supersessionism argue that either:

A. All God's promises to Israel and Judah have already been fulfilled, so there are no promises waiting to come to pass.
B. Or, that Israel has been rejected by God and the promises to Israel have been transferred to the church.

In countering these claims, we will argue that:

1. God's promises to Israel are largely unfulfilled and will come to pass in a time future to us.
2. God foretold the disobedience of Israel from the beginning and yet promised that in the last days they would be restored.

3. The New Testament again and again upholds Israel's place as God's people.

Are There Promises Waiting to Be Fulfilled?

The argument that Israel already has received all promises is simple. Some interpreters claim that all the promises of Israel's restoration were fulfilled when the people were brought back from exile and when Jesus came.

Consider some of God's promises to Israel of future hope. God said he would bring them back to the land.1 The temple would be rebuilt.2 Israel would have peace.[3]

It could be argued that these things have happened. They happened when Israel returned from Babylon.

Our argument against this idea is three-fold: (1) the return from Babylon was only a minor restoration, not the one the prophets foretold, (2) God made many specific promises that have not come to pass, and (3) even after the exile, God was still promising to bring the people back to the land.

First, consider that the return from exile was only a minor restoration and not the glorious one the prophets foretold. The number of people who returned was small. Ezra 2:64 lists their number as about 42,000. This small return could hardly fulfill God's promise that, "The days are coming...when they will no longer say, 'As the Lord lives who brought up the sons of Israel from the land of Egypt,' but 'As the Lord lives who brought up...the descendants of the household of Israel from the north land.'"[4]

Second, consider than many of God's specific promises to Israel have never been fulfilled. Consider a short list (many more could be named):

- God will make Jerusalem chief of the mountains and bring Gentiles streaming there year after year to learn the law (Isaiah 2:1-4).
- Foreigners will stream to Jerusalem daily bringing gifts to the temple of God (Isaiah 60:10-11).

- Jerusalem will become a place where people live long lifespans and where death does not occur, even amongst animal, on God's holy mountain (Isaiah 65:18-25).
- A river of life will flow from the temple in Jerusalem, make the Dead Sea alive again, and bring healing to the nations (Ezekiel 47:1-12).
- The Gentile nations will all keep the Jewish festival of Booths every year in Jerusalem (Zechariah 14:16-17).

Third, and this should be the nail in the coffin for the idea that God's promises to Israel were already fulfilled, is the fact that the very same promises are repeated after the exiles had already returned:

> I will whistle for them to gather them together, for I have redeemed them; and they will be as numerous as they were before. When I scatter them among the peoples, they will remember Me in far countries, and they with their children will live and come back. I will bring them back from the land of Egypt and gather them from Assyria; and I will bring them into the land of Gilead and Lebanon until no room can be found for them.[5]

Obviously, then, the return from Babylon was not the great promise God made (and has not yet fulfilled) to bring Israel into the land in massive numbers.

Have the Jewish People Forfeited Their Promises by Unbelief?
In counter to the claim that the Jewish people have been replaced by the church due to their unbelief we offer a simple argument. According to the Bible, from the beginning God knew of Israel's unbelief and disobedience. Yet he foretold that in the last days, they would be restored anyway:

> So it shall be when all of these things have come upon you, the blessing and the curse which I have set before

you, and you call them to mind in all nations where the Lord your God has banished you, and you return to the Lord your God and obey Him with all your heart and soul according to all that I command you today, you and your sons, then the Lord your God will restore you from captivity, and have compassion on you, and will gather you again from all the peoples where the Lord your God has scattered you. If your outcasts are at the ends of the earth, from there the Lord your God will gather you, and from there He will bring you back. The Lord your God will bring you into the land which your fathers possessed, and you shall possess it; and He will prosper you and multiply you more than your fathers. Moreover the Lord your God will circumcise your heart and the heart of your descendants, to love the Lord your God with all your heart and with all your soul, so that you may live.[6]

This prophecy of future hope was given by Moses. That means it is from the very beginning.

At the outset of God's covenant with Israel, he foretold that they would be unbelieving and disobedient. Would God then reject them? No, rather he promised in the last days to circumcise their hearts, restore them, make them more numerous than their fathers, and bring them back from the remotest lands under heaven.

To say, then, that God has rejected his people for not believing in Jesus, is saying that God's prophetic word through Moses has failed. It has not. It simply has not yet come to pass. That is why the New Testament continues to call Israel God's people.

The New Testament and the Jewish People

The New Testament is mostly written by Jews for Gentiles. Great confusion exists about the role of law in the New Testament (see my other book, *Paul Didn't Eat Pork*). Many are relatively unaware of the New Testament's teaching about the Jewish people.

The book of Romans is the primary place where Paul clarifies Israel's continuing role as God's people. Bitter rivalry between Jews and Gentiles in the city of Rome led to the writing of Romans.[7]

For the sake of simplicity, we will simply consider several clear verses from Romans 11:

- God has not rejected his people whom he foreknew (11:2).
- If the root is holy, the branches are too (11:16).
- You [Gentiles], being a wild olive, were grafted in among them [Jews] and became partaker with them of the rich root of the olive tree (11:17).
- Do not be arrogant toward the branches (11:18).
- All Israel will be saved (11:26).
- From the standpoint of the gospel, they are enemies for your sake, but from the standpoint of God's choice they are beloved for the sake of the fathers (11:28).
- The gifts and calling of God are irrevocable (11:29).

What is Paul saying?

Some claim that Paul does not mean the Jewish people. They say he is using the word "Israel" for "Christians." A different form of this argument is that Paul is only talking about Jewish believers in Jesus. But Romans 11:28, if nothing else, should set the lie to that argument. Paul is saying all these grand things about the very people who oppose the gospel of Jesus. These promises of God for a continuing place as the Chosen People are specifically for Israel in unbelief.

The exception is the promise in 11:26 that "all Israel will be saved." This promise is best taken with other prophecies to mean the last generation of Israel, the generation alive when Jesus returns. This generation, all Israel for that day, will be saved because they will believe before Jesus returns.8

The promises of God are still for the Jewish people. We do not need to try to interpret them allegorically so they can apply to the church. When God says the temple will be rebuilt in

Jerusalem, he isn't using symbolic, fuzzy language to mean that the church is the temple and heaven is Jerusalem. He means literal Jerusalem and a literal temple for a literal Jewish people.

Appendix B

Reading Plans for Learning the Old Testament

Regardless of which reading plan you choose, consider the following aids to completion and retention:

1. Ask someone to keep you accountable for your reading program.
2. Get a notebook just for this project and write a few sentences each day as a journal of your reading. It is good to include questions in your journal. At the end of your reading you may be able to go back and answer your questions.
3. Perhaps buy a new Bible for this project and highlight favorite verses and make notes in the margins or in the front pages of the Bible.

Option 1:
Read *A New Look at the Old Testament* first and then read 3 chapters a day in the Old Testament. Use a bookmark to remember where to start the next days reading. This will take the better part of a year. Refer back to A New Look at the Old Testament often to refresh your memory.

Option 2: An Abbreviated Course in Old Testament
1. First Month—Read Genesis and Chapter 1-2 of this book together.
2. Second Month—Read Exodus 16-34, Leviticus 1-11, and Deuteronomy 6-26 and Chapters 3-6 of this book together.
3. Third Month—Read Chapter 7 of this book and then read Joshua through 2 Kings. You will need to read 5 chapters per day of the Bible to finish in 1 month.
4. Fourth Month—Read Chapter 8 of this book and read Job.

5. Fifth Month—Read Chapter 9 of this book and read the Psalms. You will have to read 5 per day to finish in one month. Alternatively, you could read Psalm 1-60 and read only 2 psalms per day.

6. Sixth Month—Read Chapter 10 of this book and read Proverbs and Ecclesiastes.

7. Seventh Month—Read Chapter 11 of this book and read Hosea, Amos, and Micah.

8. Eighth Month—Read Chapter 12-13 of this book and read Isaiah.

9. Ninth Month—Read Chapter 14 of this book and read Genesis and Exodus in full. The review will be good for you and help cement what you have learned over the past 8 months.

Notes

Notes on Chapter 2
Creation and Fall

1. All of the examples regarding the use of the number seven are drawn from: Cassuto, Umberto. *From Adam to Noah.* *Jerusalem*: Magnes Press, 1978 ed. pp.13-15.
2. Pritchard, James, ed. *Ancient Near Eastern Texts.* New Jersey: Princeton Univ. Press, 1969. p.60.
3. ibid., p.67.
4. Cassuto, p.7.
5. Genesis 2:7.
6. Black, Jeremy and Green, Anthony. *Gods, Demons, and Symbols of Ancient Mesopotamia.* Austin: University of Texas Press, 1992.
7. Genesis 3:19.
8. 1 Corinthians 15:22 and 45.
9. Genesis 3:21.
10. Genesis 4:4, 8:20.
11. Genesis 22:13.

Notes on Chapter 3
Covenant Faith

1. Deuteronomy 26:5.
2. Genesis 31:34.
3. Genesis 12:1-3.
4. Genesis 11:31.
5. Genesis 26:21.
6. There is a Hittite text requiring defeated soldiers to walk between pieces of a cut-up human and animals from roughly the time of Abraham (*The Context of Scripture,*

Vol. 1, Hallo, William, ed. Boston: Brill, 2003. p.160.).
King Esarhaddon of Assyria required a defeated vassal to
appear before slaughtered animals and agree to be similarly slaughtered if failing to keep the treaty
(*Archaeological Study Bible*, Grand Rapids: Zondervan,
2005. p.1251).

7. Genesis 12:4.
8. Genesis 17:17.
9. Genesis 20:2-7.
10. Genesis 26:29.
11. Genesis 15:6.
12. Genesis 12:7, 13:18, 22:9.
13. Genesis 12:8, 13:4, 21:33.
14. Genesis 14:20.
15. Genesis 17:24.
16. Genesis 22:2.
17. King, Philip and Stager, Lawrence. *Life in Biblical Israel*.
Louisville: Westminster John Knox Press, 2001. p.361.
18. 2 Kings 16:3 and 21:6.
19. 2 Kings 23:10.
20. Leviticus 20:2, see also Jeremiah 32:35.
21. Genesis 12:4.
22. Genesis 21:5.
23. I learned this pattern of covenant threat in the Abraham
narratives from Dr. John Walton, whose commentary on
Genesis and other books on the Old Testament are highly
recommended by this author.
24. Genesis 22:12.
25. Again, this insight first came to me through a lecture by
Dr. John Walton.
26. Genesis 31:42.
27. Genesis 32.
28. Romans 11:2.
29. Romans 11:29.
30. Galatians 3:8.
31. Galatians 3:16.

Notes on Chapter 4
Bulls, Goats, and Worship

1. Deuteronomy 16:16.
2. 1 Kings 19:18.
3. Psalm 122:1-4.
4. Psalm 136:1.
5. Leviticus 23:15.
6. Psalm 122:1.
7. Psalm 84:10.
8. In the second temple, in Jesus' time, women were restricted to the Court of Women and Gentiles to the Court of Gentiles. Yet this was not God's commandment. God commanded women to bring their offerings just like men (cf. Lev. 12:6) and Gentiles also (cf. Num. 15:14).
9. Exodus 24:17.
10. See, for example, Leviticus 16:13, where the High Priest had to bring incense smoke before him to protect himself from God's presence above the Ark in order not to die.
11. Exodus 40:34-35.
12. Leviticus 16:13.
13. 1 Kings 8:10-11.
14. Numbers 19:13and 20, Ezekiel 5:11 and 23:38.
15. The rationales for the impurity laws are largely adapted from the commentary of Jacob Milgrom, *Leviticus: Anchor Bible, Vol. 1.* New York: Doubleday, 1991.
16. Ezekiel 10:18.
17. Many of the details of this chart are adapted from the commentary of Jacob Milgrim.
18. Isaiah 2:2-3.

Notes on Chapter 5
God's House

1. Matthew 27:51.
2. King, Philip and Stager, Lawrence. *Life in Biblical Israel.* Louisville: Westminster John Knox Press, 2001. p.331-332.
3. Exodus 27:18.
4. Joshua 18:1 and 1 Samuel 1:3.
5. 2 Samuel 7.
6. Deuteronomy 12:11.
7. Genesis 22:2.
8. Genesis 14:18.
9. 2 Samuel 24:18 and 2 Chronicles 3:1.
10. John 1:18.
11. Exodus 13:21 and 40:34 are just two examples.
12. Exodus 40:35.
13. 1 Kings 8:11.
14. In a letter of Egyptian Pharoah Ramses II. Cassuto, Umberto. *Commentary on Exodus.* Jerusalem: Magness Press, 1987 edition, p.331.
15. Levy, David. *The Tabernacle: Shadows of the Messiah.* Bellmawr: Friends of Israel, 1993. pp.28-29.
16. 1 Kings 8:44 and 48, 2 Chronicles 6:34 and 38.
17. Daniel 6:10.
18. Ezra 6:13ff.
19. Isaiah 2:2-4, Micah 4:1-3.
20. Ezekiel 47.
21. Babylonian Talmud: Rosh HaShanah 31b, Yoma 39b.

Notes on Chapter 6
Commandments, Law, Grace

1. Dake, Finis Jennings. *Dake's Annotated Reference Bible.* Lawrenceville: Dake Publishing, 2001 edition. p.544.

2. Matthew 5:17-18.
3. Matthew 23:2-3.
4. Matthew 23:23.
5. Romans 7:14.
6. S. Kaufman, "The Structure of the Deuteronomic Law," Maarav 1,2 (1978-79): 105-58. Walton, John and Hill, Andrew. *A Survey of the Old Testament*. Grand Rapids: Zondervan, 1991. pp.144-145.
7. Numbers 14:11.
8. Deuteronomy 1:32.
9. Deuteronomy 10:15.
10. Deuteronomy 30:12-14.
11. Leviticus 17:3-4.
12. 1 Chronicles 23:25-26.
13. Hebrews 7:12.
14. Various texts such as Ezekiel 44:10-11 affirm that Levites will serve in Messiah's temple.
15. Exodus 22:3.
16. Matthew 19:8.
17. Deuteronomy 21:10-14.
18. Deuteronomy 24:1-4.

Notes on Chapter 7
God the Warrior and King

1. This is the subject of my Master's Thesis, written in 1998 for Emory University in Atlanta. Leman, Derek. *Elisha and the King*.
2. 2 Kings 5.
3. Ruth 2:2, 4, and 4:9-10.

Notes on Chapter 8
Job, Justice, and Disinterested Love

1. 1 Chronicles 21:1, throughout Job 1-2, and Zechariah 3:1-2.
2. Other interpreters, myself included, do not think Satan is the subject of Isaiah 14 or Ezekiel 28.
3. Walton, John and Hill, Andrew. *A Survey of the Old Testament*. Grand Rapids: Zondervan, 1991. p.260.
4. Proverbs 10:16.
5. This understanding of Ancient Near Eastern religion is fairly common and can be seen by reading the myths themselves. A reader can see the same kind of theology in ancient Greek writings such as *The Iliad*.
6. The prayer, below, is from the time of Ashurbanipal of Assyria in the early 600's. This would be after Assyria destroyed Israel and before Babylon rose up to overtake them. The prayer is older than Ashurbanipal, originally written in Sumerian.
7. Pritchard, James. ed. *Ancient Near Eastern Texts*. Princeton: Princeton Univ. Press, 1966 edition. P.391. "Prayer to Every God."
8. Job 22:5-7.
9. Job 27:5.
10. Job 1:21.
11. Job 2:10.

Notes on Chapter 9
Psalms as Israel's Prayerbook

1. Walton, John and Hill, Andrew. *A Survey of the Old Testament*. Grand Rapids: Zondervan, 1991. p.276.
2. Broyles, Craig. Psalms: *New International Biblical Commentary*. Peabody: Hendrickson, 1999. pp.10-22.
3. Walton. *Survey*. p.276.
4. ibid. p.276.

5. Broyles. Pp.10-22.
6. Walton. *Survey.* P.275.

Notes on Chapter 10
Wisdom, Doubt, and God

1. Proverbs 29:18.
2. Proverbs 10:29.
3. Proverbs 1:1-6.
4. Kidner, Derek. Proverbs: *Tyndale Old Testament Commentaries.* Downers Grove: InterVarsity Press, 1964. p.58.
5. A student of Proverbs might benefit from my earlier book, *Proverbial Wisdom and Common Sense.* Baltimore: Lederer, 1999.
6. Romans 8:20-22.
7. The afterlife is not clearly taught until Isaiah 26:19 and Daniel 12:2-3.

Notes on Chapter 11
Four Prophetic Parts

1. Deuteronomy 18:15. Many take this to be a Messianic prophecy. In Jesus' day it was certainly taken this way (John 1:21, 25; 7:40). Yet, though Moses used the singular prophet, he referred not to one great prophet but to the singular office of the prophet.
2. Amos 5:24.
3. Jeremiah 2:28.
4. Micah 6:8.
5. Zephaniah 3:14-15.
6. Isaiah 30:1.
7. These four categories are adapted from course lecture material by John Walton, currently at Wheaton College in Illinois.

Notes on Chapter 12
Rend Your Hearts and Not Your Garments

1. Joel 1:8.
2. Joel 2:1.
3. Joel 2:1.
4. Joel 2:3.
5. Joel 2:12-18.
6. *Aboth d'Rabbi Nathan* IV. This is a second century rabbinic work containing sayings that did not make it into the
   Mishna.
7. Isaiah 1:12-15.

Notes on Chapter 13
Every Man a Vine and Fig Tree

1. Jeremiah 29:11.
2. See Skarsaune, Oskar, *The Shadow of the Temple*, for
   well-written examinations of the relations between
   Christians and Jews in the early centuries.
3. Romans 11:2.
4. Romans 11:29.
5. Isaiah 9:6-7; 11:1; Jeremiah 23:5.
6. Isaiah 9:7; Daniel 2:44; 7:14.
7. Zechariah 14:1-4.
8. Ezekiel 36:26.
9. Deuteronomy 30:6.
10. Jeremiah 31:33.
11. Isaiah 2:2-4; Micah 4:1-3.
12. Zechariah 14:16-17.
13. Isaiah 2:1-4.
14. Isaiah 35:1-2.
15. Ezekiel 47.
16. Ezekiel 47:12.

17. Amos 9:13.
18. Isaiah 19:23-25.
19. Isaiah 49:39.
20. Isaiah 65:20.
21. Ezekiel's promise of God's Spirit placed within Israel could be taken in other ways. It could simply mean God would give Israel a godly spirit, rather like giving a new heart. Or it could mean God would place his Spirit in the midst of the nation. It is in conjunction with New Testament truth that I interpret it to mean the indwelling Holy Spirit.
22. Luke 22:20.
23. 1 Kings 4:25.
24. 2 Kings 18:31.
25. B.T. Keth 111b. Cited in Cohen, Abraham. *Everyman's Talmud.* New York: Schocken, 1949.

Notes on Chapter 14
The Messiah in the Old Testament

1. Luke 24:45-46.
2. Psalm 133:2.
3. 1 Samuel 12:3; 16:13, and Isaiah 45:1.
4. Evans, Craig A. *Non-Canonical Writings and New Testament Interpretation.* Peabody: Hendrickson, 1992. pp.239-252.
5. 1 Chronicles 3:19; Ezra 2:2.
6. Zechariah 9:9.
7. Matthew 16:22.
8. Isaiah 53:7.
9. Many interpreters, Jewish and otherwise, deny that Isaiah 53 is about the death and resurrection of Jesus. This is a worthy debate, but for those who believe the Bible to be the inspired revelation of God, it is not difficult to make a

solid case for Isaiah 53 as describing Jesus. Other possible referents, such as Israel, Moses, or Isaiah, do not fit the wording nearly as well.

Notes on Appendix A
Are God's Promises Still for the Jewish People?

1. Deuteronomy 30:1-6, Jeremiah 23:7-8, Ezekiel 36:24-27, Zechariah 10:8-12, and many others.
2. Isaiah 2:1-4, Micah 4:1-3, Ezekiel 40-48, and many others.
3. Isaiah 2:4, Micah 4:3, Amos 9:14-15, Zechariah 2:4-5, and many others.
4. Jeremiah 23:7-8.
5. Zechariah 10:8-10.
6. Deuteronomy 30:1-6.
7. See the chapter on Romans in my other book, *Paul Didn't Eat Pork*, for details.
8. In Matthew 23:37-39, Jesus said he would not return until Israel is ready to receive him in faith.

Quick Order Form

You can order by mail or by internet. Mail-in payments must be by check or money order. Credit Card orders can be made on our website.

Mt. Olive Press
P.O. Box 659
Stone Mountain, GA 30086
www.mtolivepress.com

Mt. Olive
Press

For single copies please send $16.00 ($14.95 plus $1.05 shipping and handling). For additional copies add $15.50. Books will ship within 5 business days of your order. You may return the book for a full refund if not satisfied.

Resellers, please contact Mt. Olive Press for a competitive discount schedule.

Ship Order to:

_____

Name

_____

Address

_____

Apt #

_____

City, State, Zip

_____

Copies